UNDERSTANDING YOUR OWN
story

BROOKE LONGMORE

RANDOL WRITING
BOOKS

Published in 2022 by Randol Writing Books

Copyright © 2022 Brooke Longmore

Brooke Longmore has asserted her right to be identified as the author of this Work in accordance with the Copyright, Designs and Patents Act 1988

ISBN Paperback: 978-1-7391586-0-6
Ebook: 978-1-7391586-1-3

All rights reserved. No part of this publication may be reproduced, stored in a retrieval system, or transmitted in any form or by any means, electronic, mechanical, photocopying, recording or otherwise, without the prior permission of the copyright owner.

A CIP catalogue copy of this book can be found in the British Library.

Published with the help of Indie Authors World
www.indieauthorsworld.com

ACKNOWLEDGEMENTS

I would like to thank Neil for not only listening to all of my ever-growing ideas, but also for the support he has provided. It is a magical journey and I am grateful to have him with me on it. I would like to thank my mum and dad for their support over the years and for the encouragement to always aim higher, couldn't have done it without them. I would like to thank Justine and Lee for always being there for me when I needed them most. I would like to thank Leeson, Romi and Reeva for their unconditional love as nephew and nieces. I would like to thank Kim and Rachel for their support throughout the editing and publishing journey.

CONTENTS

Introduction	7
Chapter 1 - The beginning of the magical journey	21
Chapter 2 - Getting clear on what you want	33
Chapter 3 - Making peace with the past	49
Chapter 4 - Building a stronger life story	75
Chapter 5 - Wake up and start living	95
Chapter 6 - When it all feels stuck again	115
Chapter 7 - Trust in the journey of life	129
Chapter 8 - What comes next?	137
About the Author	143

INTRODUCTION

Psychology has always been of great interest to me. Even as a child in school I was interested in why people behave the way they do. The education system doesn't always cover such a topic, but, when we had small glimpses of this in subjects like history, studying why certain things happen in the world based on human choices, I always sat up in my chair and listened attentively. This was my passion, this was what I wanted to know more about and, still to this day, I have a hunger daily to know more and more about the human mind and human behaviour. Over the past 17 years I have been studying the science of the mind and human behaviour to fulfil this passion. I have successfully passed a number of courses from Honours degrees to diplomas, and I am constantly adding new qualifications to my list (which you can find on my website www.brookelongmore.co.uk).

Life isn't always easy, it can be extremely difficult and it can feel exhausting. Life can test us, it can have us questioning our faith and it can have us feeling defeated. We have, however, a choice each day on what to focus our attention on. Some days this will be easy and some days this will be extremely difficult.

> *"Out of the darkness comes the waxing crescent, and through difficult times you are like a light that never yields but continues to shine"*
> *- Unknown*

When I read this I thought it was absolutely beautiful, it really summed up the work that I do and how I have approached difficult times. Even during the darkest of personal times I was able to see even the smallest light, and it gave me the focus and hope that these times had come to encourage growth and the belief that it would get better, as long as I believed it could.

I started this book seven years ago, however I feel that now is the time for this book to be released. In reflection, I feel the life experiences which got in the way of this book were all for the greater good for both me and, consequently, you, the reader. All of my experiences in this time have taken me on an even deeper soul lesson, leading to me understanding myself more, which has helped my work and practices to become even better. I am in an amazing place to reflect on my journey to bring some of that wisdom your way. I am super excited to be offering this journey to you, and I hope you are too. This sentence made me smile when I wrote it, I can feel the gratitude for this book already! The term gratitude may be familiar to you, or it may be a completely new concept. Gratitude is a feeling of deep appreciation. Gratitude is a heart-based feeling and is more than just words, it is something we feel deep within us. You may want to stop for a moment or two to experience gratitude for the journey you are about to embark on. When you feel gratitude you feel better, and when you feel better you open your mind to the next chapter of your life.

Now is the right time for this book.

Throughout this book you will follow awareness steps, healing steps, engage in action steps and follow self-development exercises. When we take action we start to engage with our root chakra - our energy centre of stability and security. If we simply take in information and do nothing with it, it can quickly turn to negative thinking all over again. We have to believe in positive outcomes by taking the action, showing our mind, body and soul we know we are on the right track. When you do this, you attract back to you more of the same. A lot of people pray for a better life, yet take no action, expecting it to happen on prayer alone. We have to pray, use affirmations, hope and/or wish alongside awareness steps, healing steps and action steps. When you act, more and more doors will open when it comes to achieving your stronger story.

When I really started to feel the need to make peace with my past I was drawn to all sorts of different ideas, some of which I didn't share with others for a long time. I was around 29 when I felt a pull towards healing in the form of reiki, moon cycles and all of this stuff people call "woo woo", but for me it was starting to become fascinating and a huge part of my healing and growth process. I had tapped into talking therapies before in my life and found it very helpful, but I found that my healing felt much stronger when I mixed my action steps from therapy with spiritual practices.

The work that I offer clients covers both the eastern approach of what some call "non-conventional" therapies, such as energy healing, and the western approach of the psychological side of healing, such as talking therapies. I believe to achieve long lasting change we must focus on both. We have to work with the mind and we have to work with our body's energy to release deep traumas, unhealed heartache, disappointments, unhealthy habits and so on. It is a process of joining both psychology and energy together to achieve change that will last for a lifetime, as long as you keep working on yourself. This was not always the case as the energy healing side of therapy has only come into my life in the last 8 years. Throughout this book I will share with you the practices I have learned through my professional learning in ways that will help you to begin using the same practices in your own life. When you start to use these practices you will start to develop a sense of inner peace and will start to bring forward your beautiful wisdom from within.

> You have way more knowledge within than you give yourself credit for.

I learned in these 8 years that I was an empath and this has had its challenges, believe me. If you are an empath you will fully understand that it can be the greatest gift and the biggest curse. Being an empath means that we feel everything deeply, we are emotional and energetic sponges, and we feel the pain of others and the world if we are not looking after ourselves properly. Some people are empaths and some people are empowered empaths. I refer to myself as an empowered empath because I nurture my gifts to show-up as the best version of myself every single day. Yes, I have off days but I come back to love easily as I practice what I share in this book. It is very important for us empaths to use meditations, energy healing and so on to ensure we are keeping ourselves emotionally safe in our daily lives. This book will add tremendous value to your life if you are an empath, however it will also add tremendous value to your life if you are not an empath.

Being an empathic psychologist means I can achieve long lasting change for my clients as I work with the individual as a whole person, looking for underlying causes of the challenges that present themselves in the current day. Psychological interventions or energetic interventions on their own will only deal with parts of the challenges, bringing both of these approaches together makes way for long lasting transformational change. This is why the work I do combines both the Eastern and Western practices.

When I was a little child I used to think to myself that I would like to work with ghosts, this was the only way I knew how to describe what I was feeling. I can make sense of this now, understanding that I was interested in what couldn't be easily explained. I personally work more with the emotional mind being open to ideas, creation and sensing as opposed to logical thinking. Now, being a Mindset and Mental health specialist/Reiki Master, a lot of the work I do can be explained using theory; however, much of it requires an open mind and the whole feeling experience. Some experiences we have are purely feelings and cannot easily be explained to others, yet they have us feeling amazing! Psychology and the science of the mind is a huge part of what I do through my talking therapies, a lot of people are open to this and have known about it for a number of years. The holistic approach is becoming more and more popular, which this book will introduce you to.

There was a day where I would literally run away from people who spoke of energy healing and I say "run" away as I did! I was an academic, at this point it didn't make sense to me that there was an energy in and around us that we could not fully explain but we could feel. People told me it's like gravity, we cannot see it but we experience the benefits of it. For a while this still did nothing for me. This all changed when I hit a difficult time in my life, everything had changed and I needed answers. It is often when we are at our most difficult times in life that we feel most open for answers and the different ways they can come to us. You may have picked up this book desperately seeking answers and may be more open to hear what I say compared to 6 months ago. In my difficult time I felt myself drawn to reiki healing, angel cards, crystals and massages, the types of eastern therapies I once ran away from. I found huge comfort in these therapies and felt myself going deeper and deeper on a journey of personal healing and professional success. The more and more I worked on my energy the better and better I became at my job. For me, this was the magic of life starting to appear.

I really started to tap into the underlying thought processes that led to current day challenges. I used a mixture of psychological support alongside energy healing to take my own journey even deeper. I was on a quest to understand myself more and more. The more I understood, the deeper I wanted to go with my own journey. The more I understood, the deeper I could take my clients on their journey. They do say you can only take others as deep as you have gone and I truly experience this statement daily in my work. Therapists are limited with clients if they have not fully understood who they are, their own pain stories and how to heal them. Therapists have to work with therapists as they can only do so much on their own. In order to achieve long lasting change, we must connect with our pain stories that lie beneath our presenting problems and, as an empathic psychologist, I am able to help others daily to do this.

A little while before I was drawn to energy healing information and an understanding of the law of attraction (I will talk about this below) reached my life, I was given the tip off to read the book *The Secret*. Someone told me during a conversation where I had brought up a worry that it would be good for me to read this book because "if you think positive thoughts, you manifest positive experiences". In all my years of studying psychology this was the first time I was hearing this, at the age of 28 I had been given the greatest gift. I am an action taker so I ordered that book immediately and started to read it. You too are an action taker as you have picked up this book, perhaps you also live from the emotional mind too. You were not drawn to this book by accident.

You have been guided to this book as you want to take action, you desire to live happier and you want to feel more fulfilled.

The law of attraction is a universal law and tells us that we attract what we think about on a consistent basis. We become what we believe to be true about ourselves. You can see why so many people hit challenges in life as they have negative views of themselves which creates negative circumstances. This was fascinating for me and psychology never taught me this. Bringing together the energy work and the science of the mind work was essential from here on in to ensure I was not missing anything on a personal level, and a professional level with my clients.

Whilst reading *The Secret* I was thinking to myself, "how easy does this sound, you can simply manifest the life you want by thinking positive thoughts." I immediately followed the guidance from the book by making a vision board, introducing positive material into my life every single morning. You will find out more about vision boards, how they work and how you can create your very own vision board later in this book.

From this, a deeply held belief from years ago was brought to the surface again, I had to work on a bigger scale. This is what drove my ideas to move from working in organisations to working for myself. I knew in my heart I was restricted in organisations and would have much more freedom working for myself. I worked with a coach, used positive material, motivational speakers and a lot of soul searching to build what I have now in terms of my private practice. When we are reaching out of our comfort zone it is essential that we have a coach to support us with moving beyond the emotional blocks we often create in our minds and energy.

The information on thinking positively might sound wonderful and extremely easy; however, positive thinking alone will not work as we have to do so much more to create our destiny than simply thinking positively. We have to heal from our pasts before we can move towards positive thinking. There are a lot of limiting beliefs, negative views of ourselves and painful stories lying within us, and we must work on healing deep within, alongside our positive thinking. I will guide you through the process of coming to terms with your past in Chapter 3.

Inner child work has become a huge part of the work I do with adult clients. Most people say their childhood was fine as there were no "huge red flags", but none of us are completely safe from negative self-talk when it comes to our childhood. Many of the clients who come to me end up back in childhood due to a phrase or statement that was used in and around them during their childhood, causing challenges in their adult years. This is where viewing the person as a whole comes into play as we not only view the current challenge, but we understand what caused it, to heal it at root level.

> We must trust that we can heal in order to take our life to the next level.

When we are working through our healing we must work with our mind and our energy. We are all made up of energy. Sometimes we feel full of energy and sometimes we feel sluggish. Psychological studies tell us that some of our physical challenges are mental manifestations of emotional challenges. So, when working with energy, it is essential we work with both the human mind and the physical body. For example, some of my clients come to me sharing experiences of sore backs, sore throats and lots of aches and pains. Sore backs can often be a result of carrying too much emotional baggage around. This may seem strange at first, especially if you are hearing this for the first time; however, what the mind holds onto, the body will feel. We will not always consciously remember our traumas, but our body stores it until we heal it. Clients who are experiencing continued sore throats often find they are not communicating effectively, they are not sharing their truth or meaning what they say. Our thoughts are energy and if we are carrying heavy burdensome thoughts they will show up in our body. You have more knowledge within you than you give yourself credit for and this is another example of that. If you are struggling to understand your emotional challenges your body will be able to tell you.

Many meditations will suggest we sit still with our bodies to listen to what they are telling us.

This book will help you to develop an understanding of the mind and your energy system. When you understand both you have the power to improve the quality of your relationships, not only with yourself but with others too. This book will take you on your very own personal journey of self-improvement, see it like having a date with yourself, setting aside time to really get to know who you are.

Many adults are not aware of who they are or why they are here. You are about to understand you on a much deeper level, and this will positively impact all relationships and human interactions throughout your life.

This book will act as the initial steps towards your journey of emotional success or it may be used alongside therapy. Personal development books are a tool to use, however, they give you generic information that may not be specific to the personal challenge you are facing. When you read self-development books you may feel great, you may feel lifted and you may feel excited, however this can be short lived if you have not dealt with your emotional grief from the past. If you have read a self-development book and your upsets, traumas and worries have resurfaced, therapy is your next step. A lot of people tell me in the initial stages of therapy that they feel that they are beyond help and that no one will ever be able to help them, because they hold a belief that the personal development book they read or the seminar they attended "should" have changed their life. Personal development books and seminars are great first steps. They are great for raising awareness and great tools to use alongside therapy. But, to truly move forward we have to work with our emotional baggage on a deeper level to ensure we have removed the emotional intensity it has over our lives. This is when we truly set ourselves free.

The deeper work takes us on an inwards journey that heals our life on so many levels, which personal development books alone will not achieve. We need to use therapies such as CBT – cognitive behavioural therapy, CAT – cognitive analytical therapy, EFT – emotional freedom therapy and more. I always work with a range of therapies when working with people as this is what gets results! No doubt about it. We have to be moving forward and we have to be healing to experience long lasting change. Talking about the problem over and over will not help us to make peace with the past, it will keep us stuck. We have to be going deep within understanding our life story to make full peace with our pains. Therapy helps us to go deep within.

I have been working with and studying the human mind now for 17 years and have a wealth of experience when it comes to making positive changes in life. I have worked with hundreds of clients who were once like you are now - lost, confused, deflated and not enjoying life. Each and every one of these clients have experienced their own journey of understanding themselves better to connect more deeply with others. I have made mistakes in my life, I have had heartache and I have had tragic experiences when it comes to connecting with others; however, I have always found my way out of the darkness through using the tools I speak of in this book. I will share with you in this book from a professional experience, but also from a personal experience of living as an empath in a challenging world.

Do not be afraid when life becomes stuck again, we are always evolving, learning and growing.

This book reaches out to those who are finding relationships difficult in life. The relationships I speak of are romantic relationships, family relationships and work relationships. We will tap into all areas of your relationships to help you achieve long lasting change. You may be feeling like your relationships are tricky, like they hold you back and as though they lack meaning. Perhaps you are stuck in the negative pain cycle loop or the comparison pain loop. The negative pain cycle loop and the comparison pain loop is where you constantly compare yourself to others in a way that is detrimental to your own growth. This comparison will leave you feeling deflated and you will not take any action, believing you are not worthy of success in life. The good news is, we can work to help you understand your relationships on a deeper level by understanding you, your past emotional pain and your future desires.

Throughout this book I will be speaking of the magic in life and how we can engage in beautiful experiences on a day-to-day basis. A lot of people ignore the wonderful parts of their life, focusing on fear which they believe keeps them safe. In this book the content will help you to shift that focus to fall in love with life. You will also work on healing and releasing the past in a productive way, which will help you to move beyond challenges you have already had in life, and future challenges too.

When working through this book it would be very useful to invest in a notepad and pen. You will engage in content and exercises that will help you to really power up your wants and desires in life, and tips will be provided on how to manage life when you feel stuck again! The exercises included in each chapter will help you to get the most out of this book and are laid out in a way that are easy to follow. The exercises help you to stop and reflect on what you have learned in each chapter, and will guide you in those initial steps of really getting to know yourself. After all, you and I are working together to help make a difference in your life. Taking part in these exercises is the first step of personal development and the first step to experiencing your life unfolding in the most amazing ways. However, if you are not ready to take part in the exercises within, do not worry, you have already taken the first step by picking up this book. Go easy on yourself, do what you can do and make the most of your reading.

CHAPTER 1

THE BEGINNING OF THE MAGICAL JOURNEY

First of all, well done for making the courageous decision to pick up this book. You may have no idea in this moment just how powerful this action step is for your mind, body and soul. This book will take you on a journey of reflection, helping you to understand the relationships in your life and, in turn, give you the power to make changes. Remember, by picking up this book you are brave, you are courageous and you deserve the best life ever. I will guide you to the beginning of a new way of life.

Trust me, it happens.

Taking this back to the point of how the magical journey of life starts, I invite you to consider for a moment or two what drew you to this book? Why did you pick it up? What needs to change in your life?

The journey I will guide you through in this book may not be an easy journey. Transformation in your life involves struggle, releasing fears and, most of all, developing a deeper understanding of who you are as a person. I urge you to keep going with me through this journey. The outcome will be magical provided you follow this journey with an open mind and an open heart.

The hardest journeys in life lead us to the most beautiful destinations.

Throughout this book you will start to become grateful for your toughest times because you will come to recognise that they were a gift sent to you for personal growth. I call my tough times gifts and, let me tell you, the power in that is far greater than any challenge. To see your challenges as gifts ignites the fire within you, and this is what we will focus on throughout this book. Life can be tough and can throw us the most tragic of circumstances that cause a lot of emotional pain. We cannot control what happens in our life, but we can control how we respond to it. By controlling how we respond to life's challenges we are able to move through them with a little more ease. If you are experiencing something difficult right now, be patient with yourself as you move through this journey. If at any point the reading of this book becomes too much you are more than welcome to email me for some tips on how to manage the emotions that are coming up. Contact details of how to do this will be at the back of the book.

I sense this is the perfect time to start the journey, don't you?

It is not as simple as flipping your mindset to experience a new life. Yes, sometimes there are times a flip of the mindset will work; however, it is not as easy to flip our emotional stories or to let go of emotional pain. Emotional pain can be crippling especially if we have been faced with tragic circumstances or extremely upsetting events. From my experience, helping people who have been sexually abused, emotionally manipulated, raised by addicts, neglected as children and/or suffered a great deal of loss in childhood, experiencing addiction in their adult years, dealing with anxiety, working through grief and so on is far more detailed than a simple flip of the mindset. In these cases, deeper work is absolutely necessary for the person to feel whole again.

When a life event or person creates emotional disturbance within me, I now take a step back and ask, "What do I have to learn here through this?" Although it took years to get to this point, being here now I am so grateful I can do that and I feel strong enough to know that I have been pushed emotionally to grow through every challenge I have faced in life. Let me remind you that I am human and I do experience times where I am faced with difficult times and I find it challenging and I break down in tears; however, I can quickly move back to the energy of love and peace as I use the practices I explain in this book.

If you have ever read *The Power* by Rhonda Byrne you will know that everyone is our PETS – Personal

Emotional Trainers – meaning that everyone, even those who really upset us, are there to train us. This may be hard for you to fully accept right now, if that is the case do not worry, we have lots to work on throughout this book, do not try to force yourself to accept what you cannot accept right away. We will be looking at ways to understand experiences and people we are faced with throughout this book. You can learn to control your emotions when around others and you can learn to take every opportunity in life as an opportunity to grow and become wiser within yourself.

To make more sense of our emotional system, our physical body and how we react to certain life events I have added in a diagram I put together for my reiki trainees. This diagram will allow you to get familiar with the 7 main energy centres within our body and the way our energy system impacts our life. The 7 energy centres run from the base of the spine (root) to the top of the head (crown). When our energy centres are out of balance, our physical bodies and our emotional state will be significantly impacted. We can heal our energy centres, bringing them back into balance through therapy and through energy healing. I have placed this table at the beginning of this book for a reason.

You may be thinking why do I need to know this?

You may be thinking you came to this book to learn about the mind so why is it important to know about the energy centres within our physical bodies? It will be useful for you to have an understanding of your body's energy system as you work through this book, to start helping you connect with being in balance, and out of balance, in life. When our energy is in balance we feel great, and when our energy is out of balance we can feel frustrated and lacking in energy. The information in the table provides you with an explanation of your energy centres, what each means to you and how it feels when we are on or off track in life.

Many people who come to me for therapy have already started to take those first steps to understand their energy system, as it is spoke about more and more in today's world of self-development. This table will provide a baseline for you to understand why you may be experiencing emotional and physical challenges.

Chakra	Purpose	In balance	Out of balance
Root	Sense of security, stability, being comfortable in our own skin	Grounded, know next steps to take, belief in positive outcomes	Ungrounded, ruled by external events, negative thinking
Sacral	Emotions, sexuality, creativity	Emotionally stable, comfortable with sexuality, creativity flows	Emotionally unstable, uncomfortable with sexuality, creativity blocks
Solar plexus	Willpower, confidence, sense of identity	Focused, determined, happy with self	Distracted, lacking confidence, not comfortable with identity
Heart	The ability to love and be loved	Loves unconditionally, giving, caring	Loves with conditions, lack of compassion for others, inability to receive love
Throat	Speaking our truth	Able to put words to emotions, communicate effectively	Unable to communicate with others, not heard
Third eye	Inner wisdom	Deep sense of knowing life direction	Limited perspective
Crown	Connection to others and universe	Deeper consciousness	Spacey and head's full

Brooke Longmore, Bsc Hons, BA 2022

It's important that you have an awareness of our energy centres as we move through this book, I will refer to them at times when explaining how the mind and body work in connection with one another.

I often ask myself questions about myself and what I need to do in order to achieve what I want in life. For example, if I am trying to work on something for business and it is not happening the way I want it to, I refer to the details on the solar plexus chakra to understand where my confidence and willpower is sitting, and what needs to be worked on. I would really be asking the questions as to whether I was focused or distracted to understand what needs my attention.

How focused or distracted are you right now?

We can ask these questions when we are thinking about any area of our life. If you feel stuck, take a look at this table. Stop and take a few deep breaths before looking at the table and ask your mind to guide you to the words that need your attention. You know way more than you know. This table may start to act as a guide in life for you to see what energy centres are in balance and what energy centres are out of balance from day to day.

Is your heart and mind open to learning more about yourself?

Life can be magical, but it requires us to be open to the shift taking place. So many people only experience the struggle in life as they keep themselves so closed off from joy and happiness, or they chose careers that they think look good with no deep desire to actually carry them out. Sadness, despair, guilt, shame and much more can linger in our lives when we are feeling unhappy. The magic begins when we decide to take a step forward in life towards a transformed way of living. The magic begins when we make a commitment to ourselves to begin the process of understanding our own story. It is my hope that this book helps you to do just that. I believe we are all here for a purpose and it is our job to find that purpose to be able to live each day excited for what's to come.

Our internal stories have a lot to answer for when it comes to holding us back or keeping us stuck in life. We constantly tell ourselves stories in our mind about ourselves, our life, our outcomes, our desires, our fears and so on. Our thoughts are just thoughts, but our beliefs are thoughts we think over and over again, accepting them as true. Many people are unaware of their internal stories as they often form quickly and the mind will start to prepare for more of the same. If your internal story is a positive story then all is good; but if your internal story is a negative story you could be in trouble. Throughout this book we will be paying attention to your internal story, helping you to understand it more.

> Self-help books guide us towards challenging our thoughts.

Do you have particular self-help books you refer back to over and over again?

This book may become that book for you. Highlighting certain parts of the book or making notes as you read the book will really help you to focus in on the areas of your life that require your attention. Perhaps take a moment to reflect on the books you have read to date to understand what you have learned and why you return to them. What we focus on in life creates our beliefs and adds more information to our internal stories, leading the way for more of the same.

Our beliefs are everything and we receive what we believe in, both positive and negative.

The magic in life is available for us all, but we must align with our desires to experience the magic. In some cases, I work with clients who have gotten so used to negative thinking that it has become a habit for them, it takes up all of their head space and they attract negative experience after negative experience. Now, the good news is that habits can be changed and, with the right attitude and the willingness to change, you can turn this all around and channel your energy into positive thinking, to experience the magic of life.

Some people do not like hearing this as it creates conflict and upset within. Some people will say they did not choose the negative experience or the heartache or the job loss, but, if you take a closer look, many of your choices will have led to your experience and some of these choices have added value to your personal growth, even though they have been tough. There will still be events in your life that are out with your control but remember that you can control how you respond to your life events.

You may be starting to recognise that your journey through this book will not be easy, it will challenge you, but this is how we achieve change in our life. Challenges change us for the better, providing we allow ourselves to grow through what we go through. As I guide you through this journey, keep an open mind and remember you have come here for a reason. Some of you may have been following me on social media and feel your reason for reading this book is purely curiosity to hear what I have to say, but even still you are being guided to this part of your life for a reason.

We do not take actions by accident, we take actions that help us to grow, develop and shine!

EXERCISE 1:

Take your life to the next level:

You will need:

- Your pen
- Your journal
- 20 minutes of your time

Stop and think about what needs to change in your life. Make some notes on this before you move on. You do not have to think too hard about this, simply explore the thoughts that come up, making notes based on what comes up when you ask yourself the question, "What needs to change in my life?"

Here are some questions you may wish to ask yourself:

- What areas of my life are going well?
- What areas of my life do I need to change?
- Where do I feel in control of my life?
- Where do I feel out of control in my life?
- Where do I feel confident in life?

> - Where do I feel I hide away in life?
>
> This exercise will be your starting point for the rest of the book. Take your time with this exercise to ensure you get the most from this. If this is your first time ever completing an exercise like this be patient with yourself, there is no right or wrong way to complete this.

Remember you are stronger than you believe yourself to be.
– Brooke Longmore BSc Hons, BA

You have now started to learn more about yourself and the areas of your life that need your attention. This chapter may have been an easy read, or it may have been a more challenging read. If you wish, you can take a day or two to allow yourself to process the information you have read in Chapter 1. It is important that we allow ourselves time to process self-development material as this is where the deeper understanding comes in. Return to the book in a day or two and begin Chapter 2.

Remember you are doing great!

CHAPTER 2

GETTING CLEAR ON WHAT YOU WANT

Sometimes we are not sure of where the journey is going, but it takes us to beautiful destinations.

Let's move on to learning more about yourself and more about your life, the exciting part! The first place to start when you want to take your life to the next level is by getting clear on what you want. You will have to make peace with your past to be able to move forward successfully, but first it is important to get clear on what you want from life, that way you know what you have to make peace with to get there. Understanding where you want to go before delving in to making peace with the past saves yourself a whole lot of time. If we are all honest, we all want to save ourselves time in life. We will focus more on making peace with the past in Chapter 3, for now let's get clear on your life desires.

In Chapter 1 I spoke a lot about the magic in life and the ways in which this book will guide you through your fears, worries and troubles. Chapter 1 also gave you an introduction to your body's energy centres and how they impact the balance, or lack of balance, in your life. In this chapter we will start to look at what it is you desire from life. We will look at the areas of your life you wish to improve on and the reasons why such improvements would be exciting. You may want to refer back to the table in Chapter 1 on the chakras/energy centres of your physical body as you read this chapter, as it will give you an idea of what is in balance in your life and what is out of balance. This will also add value to your thoughts and planning about what you want from life.

> Being clear on what we want takes us to places where our soul can shine, it helps us to allow the light into our life and it helps us to experience a deep sense of joy.

Just as I was writing this sentence, the sun began to shine so strongly from behind a big dark cloud. I am taking that as a sign that these sentences hold a strong message, and that the light is being shone on us together as I write this and as you read this. I am all about signs from the universe, as you will notice as you move through this book.

Do you receive signs from the universe that help you to know if you are on the right track?

I am a morning person and always have been. In the mornings I am filled with energy and ready to take on the day. When the sun is out, I feel this even stronger. The sun is a masculine energy, which is the energy of getting things done and taking action, hence why we feel so good when the sun is out. I set up my mornings from a place of peace and always check in with my day's intentions in the morning. I would much rather go to bed early to wake up early as opposed to late nights and late mornings. I have a morning routine that I now stick to and I feel it works. When I get up in the morning, the first thing I do is journal out my ideas for the day. Being a Leo moon sign this works well for me as I am setting my intentions of how I want my day to go, igniting the fire within me. Journaling in the morning could help you to set up your day too!

Good morning routines are your key to success.

Mornings can be busy, but setting aside a little time to check in with yourself could be life changing for you. This is the difference between you controlling the day or the day controlling you.

So, what does 'getting clear' really mean then?

AWARENESS STEP 1: GETTING CLEAR ON YOUR LIFE DESIRES:

'Getting clear' is the part of this journey where you will get to know yourself more. Although there will be challenges and difficult parts of yourself and your life, you need to view it as also very rewarding. There is a lot of good that can come from looking deeply within. It is a brave journey, one that takes a lot of courage. We all have far more courage within us than we often believe. When we were little, we were very rarely taught to tap into our internal resources for strength and wisdom, so you may be learning this as an adult for the first time. We often got swept up in emotions and end up acting from an emotional place. Some adults still use the same coping skills they learned in childhood and it causes a lot of emotional disruption in their life. You can learn to change your coping skills to make better use of your internal resources of personal power, courage, strength, wisdom and a deep sense of trust that all will be okay by getting clear on your life desires.

I have witnessed transformational change time and time again in one-to-one sessions and in group sessions when people start to become comfortable with who they are. This happens when we become clear on our life desires. Initially people are extremely uncomfortable when they are asked to describe themselves. There is an uncomfortableness when the question is asked, "Who are you?"

> *Have you ever felt uncomfortable when asked about you and who you are?*

The whole purpose of this book is for you to get comfortable about who you are and we start this process when we start understanding our life desires. Often people quickly change the subject when they are asked about themselves, but in a therapy setting changing the subject does not work as the therapist will draw you right back to the uncomfortable question. You enter therapy to develop a relationship with *you*, you have to know yourself in life and your life desires to make powerful changes.

When I draw people back to the questions they are ignoring, they often laugh as they know exactly what is happening. They know fine well they have been avoiding getting to know their life desires for some time. Laughter raises the vibration and allows the client to become more comfortable looking at those deeper, darker parts where the biggest life lessons are stored. Therapy can be fun and it can transform your life. You are engaging in gentle therapy by reading this book. You are starting to ask yourself questions and will be staring to bring forward in your mind your life desires, even if you are not yet aware of this. You are showing great courage by reading this book, create space to allow yourself to feel proud of the steps you are taking. Well done, this material encourages you to ask yourself deeper questions and this is not always easy, but you are doing it!

Getting clear on what you want is to get clear on who you are and on your life purpose. That is the simplest way to put it. All changes in your life begin with *you*, therefore, to make changes, you have to know *you* and what makes *you* happy. The belief that is held by the collective is that we have to change others to feel happier, but the biggest secret is that you can change any relationship in your life by working on yourself and getting to know you.

> *You have the power to change your entire life if you understand your own story.*

AWARENESS STEP 2: UNDERSTANDING YOUR PERSONAL POWER:

Our power within is our greatest gift. It really is the part of life we are not taught within the education system. It is left up to us to learn this on our own. Before you do anything in life you must understand what you want from life and yourself on a deeper level. I have seen business owners come to me having put a lot of time into learning about business, yet only getting so far as they did not spend time getting to know themselves, they did not spend time nurturing their personal power and life desires. I have seen people move jobs, enter new relationships, move home only to experience the same unhappiness, because they did not get clear on what they wanted first. Before making any decisions on your life or your relationships, spend time getting to know yourself and getting clear on what you want. When you have started this you will then start to recognise your personal power in life and this is where you will find happiness in life.

> *Have you spent time getting to know yourself or are you simply moving from one life situation to the next without really considering what each stage means for you?*

It is essential that we spend time understanding the way we think, the way we feel and the way we act. The way we think, feel and act will impact how powerful or how powerless we feel. Much of our thinking in the early years comes from our parents and family unit. In our early years we give much of our personal power away to those around us. We want to be like the adults around us, so we mimic them and adopt their beliefs as our own. We are not aware that some of the thoughts, feelings and behaviour we are mimicking is not helping, or that some of the beliefs we are adopting and accepting as our own will hold us back massively in life. We were just innocent children keen to learn and our caregivers did the best they could with what they knew at the time. Some of the habits we have adopted from our caregivers will hold us back in our romantic relationships, in our family relationships and in our working relationships. It is now time to step fully back into your personal power, you have already taken a step towards this by picking up this book. You will hear more on this as you work through this book.

> *If you want to become clear on your life and what you want from life, knowledge and becoming an expert on yourself is the key to making powerful changes.*

I will repeat this a lot as I move through this book as it is a message we need to hear over and over. To become an expert on ourselves, raising our emotional intelligence levels will take our life to new levels.

> *Think about some of the reasons you picked up this book, what did you want to achieve?*

Much of what we learn in life is to think of others, we are very rarely taught to be kind to ourselves or to explore who we are. This has already changed for you as you are becoming more personally powerful with each word you read.

> How often did your caregivers encourage you to be kind to you as a child?

The whole message of this book is that you matter and that your life is important. This will be repeated in many different ways. What you want from life matters, your personal power matters. I do not feel this can be repeated enough to us. Everything we do in life starts with us and it ends with us.

When we truly know ourselves on a deeper level we find a new confidence for living life, we find that we connect to others on a deeper level and we find real meaning within our lives and within our relationships. This is the magic of life and we find it by understanding ourselves better. Our emotional intelligence levels increase through getting to know ourselves - when we know what we want from life, our choices become easier and our self-awareness rises. Gone are the days of taking forever to make a decision or feeling left out or feeling isolated or feeling irritated all the time. When you get to know yourself, a sense of calm will come into your life.

> We fail to trust ourselves due to life circumstances.

For example, if we hold our past traumas or we have unprocessed emotions, we often hold with it a deep lack of trust in ourselves. We fail to trust ourselves and we fail to listen to our internal guidance. When we are holding on to past hurts we feel powerless, but when we work on letting them go we step fully into our personal power.

AWARENESS STEP 3:
PAUSE FOR REFLECTION AND ASK YOURSELF THE FOLLOWING QUESTIONS:

- How do I feel about what I have read?
- What am I thinking right now?
- What am I learning about myself through checking in with how I feel and what I am thinking?

AWARENESS STEP 4:
UNDERSTANDING WHAT WE WANT TO DO WITH OUR LIFE:

We all have a deep desire that lies within us to do something in our life. We may have a deep desire to learn a new skill, become an amazing parent, to be a leader in business, to volunteer and give back. It can be anything that will make you feel happy. This is a huge question and possibly one you have never asked yourself before, so it may not come forth immediately, but be patient and your deepest desire will come to you.

Sometimes we release fears but still need to revisit these fears often. We may not clear these fears immediately as they may be held deeply within and may have a purpose at different stages of your life. If a fear continues to surface despite you having completed a lot of work around this, know and trust it has a deeper meaning and, at the other side of it, is a brand new way of being.

Being patient with yourself when you are attempting to get clear on what you want is key to the correct life purpose rising within you. Now, what I mean by this is that I have seen people over the years believe, out of fear, that their life purpose is the exact same as a friend's. Let me give you an example: I once worked with a female who came to me after getting involved in a business venture a friend had hugely encouraged them to go after. The friend was involved in this business and believed my client would be just perfect for it. Over the course of a few months the friend had pushed and pushed (client's words) my client to agree to commit to this new venture, and eventually my client felt this was their passion and they got involved. The client came to me after 2 months of being in business. Through our conversation we found that the friend's persuasion had become mixed up within my client and they had started to believe this was what they wanted, but it wasn't. We managed to work together to move the client to a place that they felt happy with.

This happens often, more often than people think. We can get so caught up in the excitement of others or the distractions that we start thinking we want what others want and we live by that, yet the deep unhappiness doesn't shift as it's not our true purpose. We may have to drop down beyond the words of others to know the answers that lie within.

During the time I started to get clear on what I wanted I started to learn many different things about my life. I really approached getting clear on what I wanted with an open mind. I was excited to learn about myself. I just felt this pull within me to strengthen and deepen the relationship I had with *me*. I had always been a kind person to others, yet at times I was very hard on myself. Although I was never hard on myself at work, as I have always had a confidence about my abilities.

How do you function in the different areas of your life?

In my personal life I can be quite hard on myself, again something I am working on all the time. Around the time I started to get clear on what I wanted, I was feeling a huge sense of wanting to be kinder to myself and wanting to really understand why I do certain things and why certain patterns play out in my life. I have learned so many deep lessons throughout my personal development, and feel I am now a transformed version of myself compared to this time 7, 8, 9 years ago. I am the same person, but a better version, and I believe we are always working on ourselves throughout our life. I approach my personal life in a far gentler way and it works well for me, but I still have to practice this a little more at times.

One of the first things I had to do when seeking clarity of what I want in life was to take an honest look at the people I surround myself with. Up until then I had spent time with people without really considering how I was being influenced by their thoughts and feelings, but the more I learned about myself, the more I started to learn about those around me. There were some people who I allowed close to me in my life that were actually not good for me at all. Cutting people off is never easy, so I had to make some challenging decisions. It is one of the biggest challenges that my clients face. We often do not want to let go of people, however, for our own personal growth, it is sometimes very important.

> *Do you find it difficult to cut people out of your life?*

It is known that we behave and act in ways based on the 5 people we spend most of our time with. How do you feel when you are with family? How do you feel at work? How do you feel within your relationship? Do the people you spend time with make you feel better, or do they drain your energy levels?

You may be noticing that getting clear on what you want is a very personal journey and it is one that you must work on by studying your external world and your internal world in some detail. Any personal development work takes some time and effort, but it is truly worth it as we move along our journey in life. Some people come so far, notice the hard work and retreat again, but those who keep going find the magic in life.

The hardest part is always the beginning of the journey as it is with everything in life, from learning to drive, to lifting weights, to meeting a new partner, to starting a new job. As you move along the journey it becomes easier, it becomes second nature and you are able to live a life on your purpose, and that is simply beautiful. Remember, you picked up this book for a reason, nothing happens by accident, therefore it is important you work with yourself to understand what all of this means for you. Most people are extremely uncomfortable in life when they are not sure of their exact direction. How do you feel when you are not sure where you are headed within conversations, within interactions and within life in general?

The focus in all therapy sessions is that the client is looking to heal emotional pain or to level up in life, but in between that time there are moments when the client is not sure where the session or conversation is going. There is part of us that has to get clear on what we want, but also to be okay going with the flow of the journey.

Your higher self, that higher intelligent part of you, will always guide you if you allow it.

Getting clear on what we want is also about working with our purpose. When we have purpose we focus our mind, and when we focus our mind we make better decisions. Getting clear on what you want is a win-win for you and will always generate good outcomes, so long as you remain focused. The world is busy and we expect everything to happen at once, so it is important that when you get clear on what you want, you also set the intention to practice patience alongside determination. This is sometimes far easier when what we want generates excitement within us, so it is really important that you really focus in on what *you* want and not what *others* want for you. We will chat more about this as we move through this book.

Remember as you move through this book to keep the focus on you. This may sound silly at first, but, if you stop and think about it, you have other people's ideas and words floating around in your mind on a daily basis. Much of our thinking comes from other people's ideas. If we are not consciously aware of the thoughts from others that we allow to become planted in our minds, we could be using up a lot of our energy on thoughts that are not in alignment with our life purpose. Some of these ideas may be limiting you massively and it is up to us to shine a light on them to release them. What thoughts do you think on a regular basis that may not actually serve you? Where did these thoughts come from? Can you let them go?

EXERCISE 2:

I invite you to stop and think about what you want in life and why. If you want to take this even deeper, it would be good to make some notes on this.

Points to consider:

- What do I want from my personal life and why?
- What do I want from my professional life and why?
- What do I want from my family life and why?
- What do I want from my relationship and why?
- What do I want from my friendships and why?
- What do I want to manifest and why?
- What do I want to learn about myself and why?

You do not have to consider all of these, pick the ones you are most drawn to and work with them, making some notes on this to come back to in Chapter 5 when we revisit this exercise.

In this chapter you have started to explore your desires in life and what you want from life in terms of personal goals. This will serve well in terms of starting to understand the next steps to take when moving along the journey of life. What have you learned about yourself from reading this chapter?

Each word, each paragraph, each chapter will take you deeper and deeper within to explore your internal world, which will have a knock-on effect on your external world. You may even be noticing light bulb moments already where you are starting to notice and understand choices you have made to date. You may have already started to explore what this means for you and how to work with this. If you haven't, that's okay, keep going. Everyone's journey will be different as they move through this book.

When I first wrote my tag line for my website '*Understanding your own story gives you the power to change it*' I was not fully sure where it had come from or what it really meant, but I had a deep knowing that I had to use it. Today I understand this sentence on a deeper level. We can only connect the dots looking back.

CHAPTER 3

MAKING PEACE WITH THE PAST

In Chapter 2 you learned about getting clear with your life desires and understanding what gets in the way of really getting what you want from life. You also began looking at the ways in which you know yourself and the ways in which you can get to know yourself even more. We have now covered the basis that life can be magical and the importance of knowing what you want from life. In this chapter we will take the next important step, which is to make peace with what holds you back from life. More often than not we are held back by our own stories. The stories we tell ourselves about our lives and the stories we hold onto from the past.

This chapter will help you to take the *initial* steps towards making peace with the past. As I have said before, it is important to remember that this book, along with other personal development books, will help you take the initial steps in understanding your life and making a change, or will act as an additional tool alongside therapy. Working with a qualified therapist will help you to heal the past on a deeper level. Throughout this chapter, I will guide you through releasing emotional baggage from the past, fears of the future and removing emotional blocks to success in life. We will look at the ways your past influences your present and the challenges within this. Our past will play a leading role in our life if we do not stop to take charge of it.

Our past will define us over and over if we do not take time to heal our emotional wounds.

Often we are unaware of what our emotional wounds are because they are hidden. The mind will deliver to us what is known as a presenting problem, behind which lies the real problem. The presenting problem is the product of the real problem. It is the problem that has been created to keep the individual safe. Read the last few lines again as it is important that you grasp this concept.

Much of our past is stored within our memory banks in the mind. Our memories are stored away with emotional intensity and will filter out into our life each time they are triggered. Emotional memories are triggered through our relationships and interactions with others. A lot of people think that putting the past behind them is as simple as just not focusing on it, but this is not always helpful, especially if there have been events that have caused emotional distress or upset. If we have an emotional memory from the past which has not yet been dealt with, a current event could cause this memory to come flooding back with a great deal of emotional intensity, meaning life becomes very, very difficult. When we heal our past wounds we start to feel clearer and we see each life event much clearer, reducing the likelihood of over-reactions.

We can take control of the mind to live a calmer life by becoming conscious of the information we absorb throughout our day.

In therapy sessions with clients, more often than not we recognise that the past is guilty of stealing or ruining the present times. The past has a loud but quiet grip over you if it has not been processed. It is quiet because you cannot see it, but it is loud because everyone else will see it in your actions. I pick up right away within seconds of talking to someone how they are feeling about themselves and their life. Past emotional pain that has not yet been processed has you living life from a huge disadvantage. You will feel exhausted, stuck, stressed, in despair, lost, unmotivated, lacking empathy, feeling too much empathy, tired and so much more.

Do you feel it is time for you to make peace with your past?

Many people are led to believe they are defined by the past and it will always impact them. This is false information. Some people will say "but that's just me" or "that's how I am built". We can change our behaviour traits if we wish to live a better, more-fulfilled life. When healing our past, therapy is like emotional and mental surgery, removing the emotional intensity that comes with the memories to live a life of peace and calm. In therapy we can take a real close look at behaviours we are not pleased with in our life in order to heal them. We absolutely need to rest when we are healing emotional pain, the same way we do when we are healing physical pain. We often do not allow ourselves the same time for emotional pain as we do physical pain, but it is vital. The mind is so powerful and, when we are making it work, we need to allow it to rest.

A lot of people think trauma is only linked with the massive red flags, such as child abuse or neglect and so on. However, trauma plays out in our life in many ways. Trauma can be the marriage breakdown, the job loss, the failed exam, parental separation in childhood, bullying, harassment, court cases, the negative words from teachers, the hurtful comments from parents and so much more. We have all experienced trauma in some way throughout life, however a large number of us never look at processing the trauma, and it continues to impact us over and over again.

Are you downplaying some of
your life challenges?

<u>CASE STUDY 1</u>
<u>SARAH AGED 33</u>

Sarah is a 33-year-old female who was experiencing huge challenges when it came to her love life. Sarah felt completely exhausted because she felt stuck in a cycle of picking the "wrong men".

Since her early 20's, Sarah found herself in numerous relationships, each of them lasting several years at a time with the same outcome in the end. The relationships continued to break down and end horribly. Sarah was desperate to find what she called "true love", but her past continued to influence how she felt about love. Sarah would watch friends fall in love and felt excited for them, but the dark hole she felt inside her, created from not having a similar love, would grow and grow.

This caused a lot of internal conflict for Sarah because she understood her friends being happy in love, but she couldn't understand why she couldn't find this type of love and commitment herself.

Sarah read book after book, completed meditation after meditation, desperately searching for "real love". Despite Sarah's efforts, the same type of man would arrive in Sarah's life, the emotionally unavailable male who would promise Sarah the world, but, after a few months, Sarah didn't see any of these promises, feeling completely let down over and over again. The cycle continued to repeat itself no matter how much work Sarah completed around self-development.

Sarah wanted more and reached a point where she had no idea how to find it. Sarah spoke with friends, colleagues and family members, yet felt that no one understood her pain as they continued to tell her that one day she would find the right man for her. This was not what Sarah wanted to hear, Sarah wanted to feel heard, properly heard, and wanted to understand why this cycle repeated itself often.

Sarah decided to engage in therapy sessions as a last resort to find the answers she was desperately seeking. Whilst in therapy, it became clear that Sarah felt unworthy of love, a limiting belief. Sarah grew up in a household that was filled with conflict and, as a child, Sarah had learned that to be loved she had to put her own needs to the side. Sarah learned that she was given attention and love when she showed up, meeting other people's needs before her own. When we looked at what it meant for Sarah to be a child, she found that no one ever asked how she was and that she was only ever given attention from parents and family members when she was helping them. Over time, this led to Sarah believing other people's needs were more important than her own, meaning, as an adult, she would give many people a lot of chances and suppress her own needs for happiness. This had led to Sarah attracting men who were selfish and who would emotionally drain her. Sarah was bringing her childhood beliefs into her adult relationships, resulting in Sarah being hurt over and over again.

We looked at these patterns and helped Sarah to unpack the emotions that were attached to the childhood memories, in order for Sarah to understand that her story was completely different now. Together we increased Sarah's sense of self-worth, helping raise her confidence levels whilst meeting her own needs.

> *This started to allow Sarah to look for emotionally available, supportive people.*
>
> *The way Sarah viewed herself after therapy was completely different to the way she viewed herself in her day-to-day life prior to therapy. Sarah eventually moved on to meet a man who she felt happy with and who was just as supportive of Sarah's needs as she was of his. By understanding her story and the impact her childhood has on her beliefs, Sarah was able to turn her whole love life around and said she felt the happiest she had ever felt.*

Can you relate to Sarah's story?

We all have a story from childhood, and a lot of the stories hold us back in our adult years. It is important we view them from a safe place to be able to understand them and to change them for our greater good.

You may be thinking of unprocessed emotional events in your life now as you read this. This example of Sarah may have triggered some events or memories that you have yet to process. If this is the case, breathe deep and know you can work on these. Exercise 3 at the end of this chapter will help you with this. Personal development books are not easy, they may trigger you or bring to the surface challenges you are not yet ready to deal with, so be patient and take as many breaks as you need as I guide you through this journey.

On the other hand, when we work with such memories many areas of our life can be positively impacted. We are often not aware of just how much negative emotional events from our past and childhood impact our entire life when they have been left unprocessed. It can feel extremely freeing when you heal your past emotional wounds, in some cases you feel like a completely new person. Whilst this book helps you to explore many challenges, this leads to a lot of freedom, so be patient with yourself and keep going!

HEALING STEP 1: THE HUMAN MIND:

Now would be a good time to explain the human mind. I have touched on this earlier when I spoke about memories being packed away in the mind, but it would be even more helpful to discuss this in a little more detail now. Again, it is not massively important that you remember all of this, it is more important that you have an awareness of the mind and how it is made up as you move through this book.

The mind is always being shaped by our experiences and if we avoid getting to know our own mind and how it is working, *it* will control *us* instead of *us* controlling *it*. It is important that we take control of the mind as it is a meaning-making machine and will look to attach meaning to certain events and situations. The downside of this is that often the meaning the mind attaches to events is incorrect.

> *Think of a time when someone you knew walked by you in the street without saying hello, what meaning did you attach to this?*

Often people jump to conclusions on the negative side (cognitive distortion i.e. Faulty Thinking) assuming that they didn't want to say hello or that they must be annoyed with them personally. The actual reality may be that the person simply didn't see you; however, we are often so quick to jump to conclusions, that we miss the obvious answer. This can also be known as personalisation where we take an event or circumstance and see it as personal towards us.

Most of the time when this happens there is a challenge within us in terms of lack of confidence or low self-esteem or lack of self-compassion. In some of these cases we may be carrying past emotional baggage that we have to make peace with. This past emotional baggage may be stopping us from seeing the truth in situations, hence why it is so important that we make peace with the past as we move throughout life.

HEALING STEP 2:
OUR SENSE OF IDENTITY MAY BE DISTORTED:

The way we view ourselves has a huge impact on how we interact with the world. The way we view ourselves forms and shapes our identity and, often, the way we view ourselves was created in our teenage years. Again, think of what was discussed earlier about how many of our habits develop in the early years of our life.

> *Do you see a pattern in the way you behave based on how you were during your teen years?*

Our identity is being shaped as we move through our teen years and much of our identity is based upon how we interact with the family unit and the way we interpret how the family views us. Notice I say the way we *interpret* how the family view us because what we do is attach meaning to events, just like explained earlier, and sometimes the meaning we attach does not serve us. We may believe people view us a certain way and create habits and beliefs based on this, although they may view us in a completely different way. A lot of our identity is based on flawed thinking and our job in the adult years is to get to know ourselves all over again from a more intelligent place with more emotional awareness. It will be important to understand your sense of identity, how this sense of your identity formed, what parts you need to change, and so on. This will include healing emotional stories of how family members treated you or how the family as a whole treated you. When we are looking back at our upbringing it is important that we understand what went on around us and how we felt about it. I will guide you to this emotional awareness throughout this book.

HEALING STEP 3: UNDERSTANDING THE MIND AND HABITS:

Our minds are made up of our conscious mind and our subconscious mind, you may have seen the iceberg image of this on the internet or on social media.

Conscious mind (10%) controls:

- Short term memory
- Critical thinking
- Logical thinking
- Willpower

Subconscious mind (90%) is our:

- Beliefs
- Habits
- Emotions
- Values
- Protective reaction
- Long term memory
- Imagination and creative thinking

You can probably see now that the subconscious mind basically rules the show as it makes up a large proportion of the mind. We feed our subconscious mind information based on what we listen to or watch or believe to be true. A lot of our beliefs that are held within the subconscious mind began in our early years of life. The subconscious mind is like a computer and it will run our lives for us based on the habits we engage in.

We can at any point change our habits if they do not serve us. Remember, most people go about their daily morning routine without having to think of it. When they first started, they would have had to think about it to create the routine, but over time it became a habit and most people will go about their mornings like a computer, never really stopping to think of what they do and if it serves them. To make peace with our past we have to stop and really think consciously about our actions, our habits, our beliefs and so on. Our habits are not stuck, they can be altered and changed to be brought into alignment with our life desires. For example, a person who has not had a great experience of love in their life may look to understand their habits and thoughts around love. This person may want to start by developing healthy habits of self-love and self-care, taking time out to look after themselves. This in turn will help the person to feel more love and will help them to attract more love.

> *Do you have any idea how many times a day you are triggered by past emotional pain?*

HEALING STEP 4:
TRIGGERS FOR PAST EMOTIONAL PAIN:

You may have no idea how many times throughout the day unprocessed emotional pain is being triggered; however, you will feel this in your body as tension, stress, tiredness, irritability and lack of focus. If you are feeling any of these feelings on a regular basis, chances are something is going on within that needs your attention. If this goes on for a period of time physical illness may manifest as a result. Your body will always guide you on what you need to know about your emotions. It is important that you stop and listen often throughout the day. Throughout this book I will provide you with the tools to encourage you to stop and re-evaluate your daily habits and daily actions.

> *Do you gift yourself the time of stopping throughout the day?*

It is really helpful to give yourself time each day to process how you are feeling, this creates space for a deeper understanding of ourselves during our periods of healing. Healing is like a cycle we go through, it is part of our life journey and there is lots to be learned during the cycle of healing. I check in with how I am feeling each morning when I am starting my day, in the mid-afternoon usually around 3pm, and again at night before bed. It is good to develop a habit of checking in with yourself several times each day to ensure you are aware of how you are feeling, so if anything needs your attention you will be able to step into your personal power and deal with it. Slowing down and tuning in is your key to emotional success.

HEALING STEP 5:
THE MOON CYCLE AND EMOTIONS:

I felt very drawn to slowing down and tuning in with the energy of my body and the energy around me during my time of healing. When I wanted to make full peace with my pains I started to work in alignment with the moon cycles. The moon impacts our mood because it draws on our energy, like it pulls on the tide, as we are made up of water. The moon is being spoken about more and more these days as we move forward to a deeper level of understanding of its power, you may have seen movies display the heightened emotional states in people around the time of the full moon.

I have had teachers come to me to explain that children's behaviour is always far more extreme around the times of the full moon. The teachers who have come to me have wanted to know more about how to support this heightened behaviour in the classroom. The behaviour they often see around this time is increased moodiness, increased anger and increased emotional outbursts. Adults will often share with me challenges in their relationships around the time of the full moon, such as difficulty communicating with their partners, challenges around sleeping and tiredness, and challenges with mood changes. We are all impacted by the moon cycles and having an awareness of this will be really helpful for you throughout this process of getting to know you more.

> *Have you noticed any mood changes within yourself around the time of the full moon?*

The healing journey is not easy and it is always good to have someone by your side to guide you through it. I would always suggest to keep an open mind when on the healing journey, as a closed mind will really prevent the positive work from taking place. I found my healing went deeper when I started to work with the moon cycles as I started to go with the flow of life. I started to work with the law of attraction. I started to co-create with the universe and, by coming on this journey with me, you can too. I am writing this section of the book at the time of the full moon, and I have been working on big emotional releases and letting go of people and situations that do not serve me. Many of the clients I work with are drawn to working with the moon cycles as part of their healing.

The full moons are a great time to release that which no longer serves you and there are lots of exercises you can do around the times of the full moon to release old, stagnant energy. It is a great time to make peace with the past and to use that heightened energy to release old, out-of-date emotions. We can never really move forward until we have healed our past, as you have read throughout this chapter. There are exercises we can engage in at the time of the full moon to fully understand our emotional state and how to work with this.

> ### EXERCISE 3A, FULL MOON EXERCISE:
>
> On the day of the full moon I invite you to take your notepad and pen and answer the following questions:
>
> - How am I feeling today and why?
> - What do I need to let go of to feel more in alignment with my life desires?
> - What action can I take that will help me to move forward in the direction of my life desires?
>
> This exercise will help you to understand yourself better, to release old emotions and to move in a new direction feeling empowered. You can do this exercise every time we have a full moon. I have a moonology calendar in my office to remind me of the moon cycles and to keep me on track as I work with the moon cycles every month.

There are times where people become rigid and resist change, which creates tension and challenges.

HEALING STEP 6: CHAKRAS:

Another way you can understand your emotions and make peace with the past is to have an understanding of your chakras. If we think back to the chakras mentioned in Chapter 1, the root chakra is important when we are thinking of change. Many people have a history of fear or survival mode, meaning their emotional and physical bodies are stored with trauma around the base of the spine, making it harder to know what steps to take to move forward. We hold a lot of our trauma in our bodies, hence why we see so many benefits being shared by yoga practices, meditation practices and breathing practices these days. We will look at meditation more in Chapter 4. I remember, following a really difficult time in my life, doing yoga and when I was practicing a particular pose I started to cry, and I mean *really* cry. It was like any emotions that were stored in my body from this time were being released through my awareness of that part of my body. You will not be surprised to know it was a hip opener exercise that caused this emotional release. Hip opener exercises in yoga engage with our root chakra, releasing any built-up fears.

> After it I felt great.

The trauma and fears we hold on to may have been with us for many years, some since our childhood.

> Do you hold on to any fears from childhood still today?

HEALING STEP 7:
YOUR CHILDHOOD STORY AND ATTACHMENT THERAPY:

The child who was always criticised and felt the need to please the parents constantly to receive love, will be the adult who is struggling in personal and romantic relationships. Healing needs to take place. This adult learned as a child that to receive love perfection must be achieved. Now, most of us know this is not possible, therefore, what the person is looking for is not going to happen, meaning they are chasing a fantasy. For this person, attachment therapy will be a great therapy to understand how to positively and securely connect with others, releasing the need for perfection. Personal development books alone will not heal childhood trauma such as attachment issues, we often need to tap into therapy on a one-to-one basis at the same time as we educate ourselves on the topic.

I must make it clear when we engage in discussions during attachment therapy we are not looking to blame the adults who raised us, as they were only doing the best they could at that time. We are simply looking to understand and to change our current behaviour patterns to make peace with our past, to ultimately find happier and more fulfilling relationships with the people around us. I have had clients come to me in this exact situation and, the minute we start unpacking these emotions through talking therapies, tears run and run and run as there is so much emotional build up that has been stored in there for years. There will be a lot of emotional dust and a lot of cleaning to do, maybe call it a spring clean of the mind and body; however, when you do this, life becomes clearer and you can make peace with your past.

> *You will start to see all areas of your life in a completely different way. You will see love that you never saw before.*

You will see beauty that you never saw before. You will see excitement that you never saw before. Life becomes magical.

HEALING STEP 8: ATTENDING THERAPY:

Another excellent way to make peace with your past is through memory recall work in therapy. Now, this is not great to do at home as you may open up memories that are overwhelming. It is always best to do this work in therapy as your therapist will remain present, guiding you through what you need to learn to set yourself free from the past. You can do this at home with meditations, but, like many things in this world, it is far safer to engage in this type of therapy alongside a trained professional.

I must add there are some exercises you can do at home on your own to take the first steps towards understanding and making peace with your past. The first one being working through this book. The second being taking part in the exercises at the end of each chapter. These exercises will be your initial steps towards healing. This book raises awareness of who you are as a person, whilst teaching you the workings of the mind. These are fantastic first steps, even if you do not enter a therapy room. Those who feel ready for lifelong transformation will take further steps towards this after reading this book, and some of you may even start this process of greater healing whilst reading this book by booking a therapy session.

> *It is important that you follow the journey you are most comfortable with, but it is also important that you push yourself out of your comfort zone.*

When we are faced with a challenging life event, we store this life event in the memory bank of our mind and attach to it a lot of emotions felt in that moment. When we are faced with a similar life experience, these memories come flooding back through a process called 'mental filtering'. What is happening here is your mind is now filling in the blanks of the current situation with data from the past, creating more of the same. The huge issue here is this current event only has to mirror a *slight* part of the past event for the mind to flood this information through, this being the reason people live the same painful experiences over and over again.

> *Have you been living the same pain loop over and over again?*

When faced with a life event that looks like a past event, there could be a whole new reaction to the event, a more mindful reaction, but this will only happen if we have healed the emotional memory, which we can do through memory recall work in therapy. We bring the memory back following a meditative/hypnotic state being achieved. When we bring the memory back, we start to unpack the emotions attached to the event, taking the emotional intensity out of the memory. We are then able to change the way the mind views the memory through positive suggestions. This frees the person of the emotional challenge and allows them to approach a similar life event in a completely different way.

You can begin to take the first steps towards working with this by becoming conscious of how you respond to life events. Start to connect with your mind and body as you read this book.

These are your initial steps to making peace with the past. We have looked at triggers for your emotions based on past experiences, chakras and the connection to our emotions and we have looked at attending therapy. Start to recognise the life events, the people, the situations that cause you upset and, by recognising these patterns, you may discover the pain that you need to make peace with from the past.

Let me give you an example of this.

CASE STUDY 2
LORNA AGED 29

Lorna had been on the receiving end of what she called 'nasty' treatment from her boss. This was impacting Lorna emotionally and she felt on edge around this person constantly. Lorna described it as being in constant fight or flight mode. It was exhausting and she was always feeling physically stiff with aches and pains.

Lorna felt that her future was at risk as a result of the treatment from the boss and the emotional memory, although she was not as conscious of the control the memory had over her until I had pointed this out. Many people are not consciously aware of how much control an unprocessed emotional memory can have. We had to sort this out.

We agreed that memory recall work would be the best approach for this. We worked with the memory of the most significant event, drawing on all details of the challenges etc. We spent time healing the memory using analytical techniques and also healing suggestions. Lorna described the hurt and the anger as being lifted at the end of the session. Lorna shared with me she felt free from this event. By understanding and unpacking the event, we had removed the emotional intensity from the memory, taking away its control. The memory recall session had been a success. These controlling, emotional memories happen more often for people than they think, it can even be one event that clogs up your whole emotional system. If you want to see us humans like cars, it is important that we have a regular MOT to set us free from that which holds us back.

Can you relate to Lorna's story?

It surprised me in my early years of working with and studying the human just how much one small event can cause so much pain for individuals if it has not been processed.

It can be something you may not even remember that is causing all of your emotional challenges. We work in therapy to bring this to the surface, to let it go. I do this by knowing the right questions to ask based on the information my client gives me. More often than not the client is shocked by what has been holding them back for many years, it may have been an event that went unnoticed but caused years of struggle.

You will now be recognising there are many ways we can make peace with our past. From this chapter, you will also recognise the importance of making peace with your past to live an emotionally successful life. You have started in this chapter to understand the mind a little more which will be helpful in terms of making peace with the past.

What have you done to heal from your past since you picked up this book?

You will be able to make small changes at home using this book, however engaging in therapeutic programmes will bring about long-lasting and truly transformational change. The reason for this is that therapy creates a space to work on what you normally resist. In therapy we create the space to work with the emotional memory, to unpack it without distractions, to remove the emotional intensity for good, and to ensure it no longer controls you.

You can start at home by becoming conscious of how your body reacts to certain events, check in with yourself regularly throughout the day and ask yourself, "how am I feeling right now?" It may be that every time you are to attend a works meeting you feel really tense, this may indicate unresolved emotions related to power and authority are taking control. It may be every time you see your parent, you leave feeling bothered. This may indicate that there is attachment work needing to be completed. Remember, we each have our own story to process and understand, which you can take the initial steps towards by engaging with the information and exercises in this book.

The following exercise will help you to start identifying what needs your attention.

EXERCISE 3B:

Before moving on, start to recognise unprocessed events that are causing disruption for you.

- What emotional pain from the past do you feel gets in the way of your life desires?
- What events from your past still cause disruption within your life?
- Are you noticing times when you are emotionally triggered?

The answers that may be presenting themselves from these questions may be intense, therefore therapy or healing work is coming to mind for you. Recognise the areas of your life that you need to make peace with and take action to start the healing process now! You may want to make notes on this to make it clearer.

Good luck!

CHAPTER 4

BUILDING A STRONGER LIFE STORY

In previous chapters we have looked at the magic in life and the ways in which you may be ignoring the good in your life. We have looked at getting clear on what you want, and we have looked at making peace with the past. I will now guide you through the process of building a stronger story. In this chapter we will look at what it means to show up in life in a more meaningful way. We will also look at the meanings we attach to certain life events and how different meanings may be holding you back. Lastly, we will look at the initial steps you can take to start to build your stronger story.

This chapter is filled with action steps for you to take to build your stronger story. It is best to read through the chapter as a whole and then engage in the action steps through exercise 4 at the end of the chapter. Exercise 4 will guide you to stop and work on each action step before moving on with the book. This allows for time to process each action step before engaging in the exercise.

This is the part where you can really tap into your creative wisdom. Before working on this chapter, it is important to have worked through the material in Chapter 3 on releasing your past.

If you have not yet healed past pain it will get in the way of what you are trying to create. This is why you may have at times felt unable to write the book, unable to create the website, unable to find the words for your social media post, unable to communicate your love for your partner, unable to share your grievance at work, unable to discuss your true feelings with your family members and so on. To really create a stronger story we have to set ourselves free from what is holding us back. We do not have to have dealt with every single bit of our emotional pain, we simply have to have started dealing with and facing the parts of our emotional pain that stand in the way of our life desires.

Whilst I am writing the start of this chapter, I have the most beautiful candle burning in the room. This candle was a gift from a lifelong friend of mine, Donna. I had always liked the smell of the candles in her house and as a surprise she bought me one for my house. I thought it was a lovely gesture and one that has made me feel very special. Justine (my sister) and I have been friends with Donna and her sister Claire since childhood, so we have so many positive memories to look back on. Every time we meet up we chat about the same memories and laugh even more. Who pops into your mind when you read this? What family members or friends have given you gifts recently that have meant a lot to you?

When we surround ourselves with positive people anything is possible!

It is so important when we are looking to build a stronger story that we have people around us who care about us. This point I cannot stress enough. Humans are built for connection, we come into the world ready for it and we always live life in a much better way when we feel connected with others. The content in this book is helping you to connect more deeply with others.

The relationships we have in our life can be our biggest source of joy or our biggest source of pain.

When we are not feeling good within ourselves or when we are feeling confused, drained, stressed, anxious and so on it can be difficult to see the positives in our life, such as the people around us, or, on the flip side, we make poor choices about who we have around us.

Possibly when reading this you may have started to think of positive people from your childhood who shared great times with you, or perhaps this story highlighted a gap in your life. Whatever has come up from reading this, sit with it for a minute before moving on, ask yourself what your emotions are telling you. If they are happy memories, what is the message for you. If they are sad memories, what is the message for you? You will now be understanding that I encourage pausing and reflecting and getting to know yourself a lot, because I believe understanding your own story first gives you the power to change it.

When you feel ready to move on again, let's go!

As I've said before, we are meaning-making machines, we want to put meaning to events, people, circumstances, etc. in our life. I am forever looking to understand the meaning of events in my life. Being an empath means we experience the meaning of life on a much deeper level. I have worked through a lot of my emotional pain to be able to see life events and the meaning of life clearly. Neil (my other half) will tell you that I am always sharing the understandings I come up with when I search the meaning of life. I'm lucky he's a good listener as I can sure talk! When we put meaning to events, we understand them, and when we understand them, we can process them. Remember, it is important to ground ourselves when attaching meaning to events and people, as this will help us to see things clearly. Grounding techniques can be deep breathing, sensing your surroundings and tuning in with your emotions, before jumping into making a decision on the meaning of an event. Processing is a practice of patience and really tuning into yourself, this is what helps you to build a stronger story.

Do you feel like you are always moving from one place to the next in life, possibly feeling constantly anxious?

It really helps to slow down in life, and to listen to and work with your emotional guidance system. Chances are you are not processing life events in a helpful way because you have never been taught how to. Events, people and circumstances in our lives are always teaching us what needs our attention or what we have to move away from. But, if we are not slowing down enough to listen to our inner intelligence, we could be causing ourselves a lot of emotional disruption in life. Slowing down takes practice and it takes time.

This is the foundations of a stable and secure life. I like to call it an emotionally successful life.

<u>CASE STUDY 3</u>
<u>TOM AGED 35</u>

Tom came to me for support as he had experienced a great tragedy in his life, the death of a parent.

This had come very suddenly for Tom and his life had been impacted significantly with this bereavement. The work Tom and I did helped Tom to slow down and to tune in to his emotions, because this was the first time he had been faced with such tragedy and he had never engaged in therapeutic work before now.

We worked through, week by week, looking at the emotions that were coming up for Tom and exploring them in more detail. Some weeks we had to work on an action plan for Tom to use when around other family members. A lot of my clients who come to me for grief work explain how they feel misunderstood and that others make unhelpful remarks, not understanding or knowing what to say.

Tom felt much more able to focus on his own life after his therapeutic journey, because, as he shared, he felt much more in control of his grief.

> *The reason I share Tom's story is to generate hope as sometimes the greatest tragedies in our life also create space to explore ourselves on a deeper level, which in turn helps us to build a stronger life story.*

Can you relate to Tom's story?

In this chapter we will really tap into your creative side and the pleasures of life, to generate excitement, hope, happiness and inner peace – building your stronger life story.

When we are stuck in emotional pain or emotional challenges, our creative side becomes numb and it's often very difficult to think outside the box. We are here to enjoy life and we can become the author of our life, creating what we want and creating magical experiences that make our heart chakra sing (refer back to the table in Chapter 1 if you wish to remind yourself of the heart chakra).

We can create a completely different future for ourselves.

We always have the opportunity to build a better life for ourselves, we do not need our lives to look like they did in the past. Creating our new story is exciting. We feel free when we are open and ready to create. There are many ways we can create a brand-new story. Our mind works in habits, it is up to us to feed our mind new habits to reinforce the new life that we want. We have to repeat over and over again, affirming to the subconscious mind the new life that we want. We want to see things in our world that mirror the new life and say yes, yes, yes to it. There are many practical tasks you can try at home to get you started on your creation journey and to help you build your new, stronger life story, some of which we will explore in this chapter.

Here are some of these tasks:

- Daily meditations

- Journaling

- Deep breathing work

- Spending time in silence

You may want to revisit the exercise from Chapter 2 before moving on again as it will be really helpful for this stage of the book. In Chapter 2 you started to think clearly about your life desires. Sometimes we can get a little lost from our life desires and it is helpful to remind ourselves of our wants from life often. Every time we remind ourselves of our life desires, we realign with our life purpose.

Building a stronger story takes perseverance and commitment. It is not an easy step, however, if you are clear on what you want and what you want excites you, then it will be much easier to take action. Again, remind yourself to follow your own heart when it comes to taking action.

The mind works with what we feed it, therefore, when you are looking to build a stronger story, you are going to want to surround yourself with reminders of what you are trying to work towards. When I say what we feed it, I do not just mean food, I also mean the information we focus and concentrate on. For example, if you are looking to start running to feel more fit and healthy, you will benefit from having items, for example images, around the house that reminds you of your goal. You may wish to pop your running shoes at the door to make sure this is the first and last thing you see when you enter and leave the house. This will continuously send a message to your mind that you are a runner and you will start to think like a runner and act like a runner. The more you see your reminders, the stronger your mindset around your desires will become.

If you want to build a stronger story, yet you surround yourself with people who complain or you live in an untidy environment or you watch negative programmes all day, you will not succeed. You have to consciously think from now on about the information, conversations, and environments and so on that you are exposing yourself to. Your conversations and the information you engage with are all sending messages to your mind, and the mind will start to create thoughts and feelings based on what it is fed. Make sure you start to really think about the choices you are making and whether or not they are aligned with your desires and life purpose.

My environment in my house is filled with positive quotes, crystals, colour and candles. These act as constant reminders of my desire to feel at peace and to feel comfort in life. It also reminds me that it is important to slow down and to check in with how I am feeling. There is not a day that goes by that I do not create some time for myself to check in with me. I am surrounded by reminders and this has become habit for me.

Look around your environment, what do you see? Does what you see make you happy? Could you bring more happiness into your environment?

The mind works in habits and habits will form very quickly, both positively and negatively. Therefore, it is up to us to create good habits by surrounding ourselves with information that feeds those good habits. When we are building a stronger story, we are re-writing our life stories, so it is important we develop patience along with the excitement of new beginnings. Patience along the way allows us to build a strong foundation for our new story, and this is what we need for it to be a success. It is never too late to build a stronger story.

No matter how tough it is or how tough it has been, we can always build a new story for ourselves.

A lot of people believe that they are really stuck in life, and they cannot build a stronger story, or that their future has to look just like their past. However, this is not the case because in every given moment you can choose to live a completely different life, and that is what we are focusing on in this chapter. Keep trusting that everything is working out for you and that you can continue to heal as you move through this journey. It is a journey and it will continue to unfold bit by bit, keep trusting. Building a stronger story will take practice too, as this may not be something you are used to.

When I was starting to really delve deep into my personal development journey, I had a lot to work on before building a stronger story and this has had its ups and downs along the way. There was a lot of healing required in the initial stage, and a lot of revisiting of healing as I moved along the journey. To be able to build my stronger story I had to let go of a lot before I could move forward. You may be noticing here that much of building your stronger story is still about healing and making peace with the past. You may have thought that part was over after leaving Chapter 3; however, to really build a strong, positive life, you will have to continue to be willing to heal as you move along. Life keeps evolving, we are always growing, we are always developing, and we are always healing.

Have you been allowing your healing to take place as you move through this book?

Are there any parts of your healing journey you have been resisting?

Again, you may want to revisit the notes you made at the end of Chapter 2 or at least keep them in mind as you move through this chapter, as you will be building on and putting the ideas from Chapter 2 into action. This is the stage where you will be looking at putting your desires and what you want into action steps. Reminding yourself, as much as you can, of what you desire and what you want will be your key to success in this area. This is the part of the puzzle where you start to take action of what you really want and not what others want for you, because this is *your* very own life story and it is *yours* to live.

In summary so far, if you wish to build a stronger story you have to surround yourself with reminders of your new story, you have to have made peace with negative emotions, you have to be open to more healing, and you have to be ready for action steps.

I think this is the right time to start looking at the action steps you can take to build a stronger story, so get excited, let's go!

ACTION STEP 1: VISION BOARD:

The first action step you will want to work on when building a stronger story is creating your vision, which you can do by designing a vision board. If you require further assistance with this, please remember you can reach out to me for further guidance to get you back on track. I mentioned earlier in the book just how helpful vision boards are when it comes to living your best life. I have been using vision boards now for about 7 years and I have benefited hugely from designing my vision board. Vision boards are a must!

When making your vision board you may wish to pop on good music. Music is a fantastic way to raise your energy levels and you will want your energy to be high when you are putting together your vision board. Music for me is more than just music, it moves my soul. Being an empath means that not only do I listen to music, but I feel it too.

So, what is a vision board then?

A vision board is a board that you will place images and words linked to your desires on. This board will then be placed at a central point within your home, somewhere you will see it often to act as, not only a reminder, but a tool for programming the mind. The mind will work to bring to life what it is exposed to on a regular basis, so your vision board will act as a reminder for your mind and the images will become something your mind seeks to find.

To make your vision board you will need a cork board, pins, images and words. When you have all that you need, the exciting part starts by placing your images and words on your vision board and placing it somewhere you will see it often. Your vision board will programme your mind to bring people, events, situations and experiences into your life, to build your stronger story. I have pictures of a house I want to buy and ideas for my business on my vision board. I also have some images of chakras and words of feelings I want to experience placed nicely on my vision board. A mixture of words and images are great as the mind will work with both. If you need additional ideas for this you may want to look online at examples of vision boards. When you have a desire you wish to bring in to your life it is very helpful to have it on paper, because the mind understands this as committing to your desires.

Many of my clients over the years have created vision boards and have found the results to be absolutely amazing. One client in particular of mine had a business vision board and placed this in their working space where they could see it often. This acted as a reminder of what they wanted in their life when times were tough. My client shared with me that their vision board helped them to take action when their mind was throwing negative thoughts at them. Their vision board was a constant reminder of what they were working towards and helped them to commit to their goals.

A vision board fires up our determination when we feel like we are lacking or when we feel like we are falling into the trap of people pleasing. Our goals are very closely linked with our solar plexus, which you would have read about in chapter 1. Our solar plexus is our energy centre of personal power and the fire within. Our solar plexus energy centre deals with our boundaries, determination and our ability to get things done. Our solar plexus also deals with our sense of identity and how we view ourselves. A vision board helps us to maintain good energy in and around our solar plexus to take consistent action. The reminder of what we desire continues to feed that fire within, helping us to take the action steps needed to push through the moments we are second guessing ourselves or feeling tired.

Good luck with your vision board and remember I am here to help you!

ACTION STEP 2: MEDITATION:

Our stronger story is built much easier when we are reprogramming the mind to believe in our stronger story. Meditation is another great way of reprogramming the mind. Now, many people will say they cannot meditate, but they can. Believing you cannot meditate is the biggest block to meditation and it is simply not true. You are in a meditative state every time you focus all of your attention on something.

> *Many people are in a meditative state when watching the news.*

They are listening to every word, eager to know what is happening in the world, believing every word to be true and accepting it as so. This is meditation. I don't watch the news as I feel it is very negative and for an empath the news can be emotionally unsettling, so it is something I stay away from.

> *Let's learn how to meditate!*

I am going to explain to you the simplest way to get started on meditation to help you out if you are someone who feels they cannot meditate. When you are meditating, it's important that you work with meditations that are in alignment with what you want from life. You might want to have your notes close by that you made in Chapter 2.

You can use YouTube for meditations. I prefer YouTube to the apps for meditation as the selection of meditations is much greater. When I'm about to meditate I always think of what I'm trying to achieve and what I'm working on that week for my life desires. For example, if you have a desire to feel more confident when public speaking, you may wish to work with throat chakra meditations or confidence affirmation sessions.

When you are meditating, find a comfortable place in your house where you can sit or lie down. The meditations often guide you on the best position for each of them. My best place to meditate is my bed, although I do fall asleep a lot when I do. It's perfectly okay to fall asleep when meditating so do not worry. Sitting up you can avoid this though if you wish to be present, for example when meditating during the day.

Here are some tips on starting your meditation practice:

- Go easy on yourself, remember it's not a race, it's all about practice
- Use the same meditation for a period of 21 days to practice over and over, before changing to another meditation
- Use short meditation sessions, perhaps 10 minutes
- Meditate at the same time, every day, in the same place, i.e. your armchair every day at 7pm

The reason a good meditation practice is helpful for beginners is that your mind will start to work with the habit you are creating, and it will start to realise that this is your chill time and will learn to calm down much easier each time. You may also wish to start a meditation diary, keeping notes of your meditations. You may wish to note down how you felt or you may wish to note down any emotions that came up afterwards. Again, for first time meditators it's good to really tune into your practice by giving it your attention. Don't worry about getting it perfect, it's more important you factor it in regularly and practice, practice, practice. Meditation will also take your spiritual practices to the next level, helping you to become more intuitive.

You will be noticing with the chat of visions boards and the focus on meditation that changing your life and building a stronger story will take practice and time, something you are reminded of constantly throughout this book. The reason I repeat this so much is that it can be so easy for humans to lose sight of the good they are doing, turning to critiquing themselves which can lead to results unravelling. When we remind ourselves practice, patience and good habits are the key to success, we give ourselves a much better chance at building emotional success.

There is no time like the present – start meditating!

ACTION STEP 3: MUSIC:

When building a stronger story music is also important. Words have a vibration and it's important that we are conscious of the words we listen to on a regular basis.

Most people have a playlist, yet they are not conscious about their playlists. Words will trigger us without us knowing or realising at times. For example, it may be that you cannot understand why you cannot move beyond your recent heartache, yet the music you listen to speaks of long-lasting heartache, which activates your heartache over and over without you realising.

If you have never saw the effect of words on water you may want to go and watch that now on YouTube to see just how much of an impact some words have. Different words have different vibrations and, again when building a stronger story, we want to ensure we are exposing ourselves to words that match our desires as much as we possibly can. Make it your task to put together a playlist of around 20 songs that ignite the fire within you and listen to this playlist often.

I remember when I was working for organisations but wanted to be self-employed I had a playlist I listened to over and over. The songs all had meanings of working from home or being free. Every time I listened to this playlist I would visualise myself working from home and living my brand new story. Now, any time I hear those songs I still smile as they will always be a huge part of my story! After all of these years the songs still hold meaning for me and take me back to this exciting time where I literally programmed my mind to believe I could work at home for myself.

You are starting to become aware of the tools you can use in your life to build your stronger story, such as vision boards, meditation and music. Anything I ask my clients to do are all things I do myself to keep building my own stronger story.

> *I know and understand how tough it can be to build your stronger story, but with persistence you will get there.*

You have now started to take the steps towards building a stronger story. It is important you continue to do this throughout the book. Your story will continue to build as you continue to take action. You have looked at creating a vision board, taking steps to start meditating and have also looked at the power of words. By following each action step you will begin to live an emotionally successful life.

You will be starting to notice that building a stronger story will take a lot of work, but it'll all be worth it. Reading this book will help you to raise your awareness and understanding of the mind, but the action steps are the part that will help you to experience the magic in life that was spoken about in chapter 1. You may have been feeling already that this book has spoken to you in certain ways and, when this happens, it is important you follow this up with action. Information mixed with action is where it all happens. Remember in chapter 1 I spoke about in the midst of discomfort, like you may be experiencing going through this book and coming to terms with your past and life desires, your heart is still opening if we allow it? This is the point where I remind you to allow it by taking the action steps I speak about. Make your vision board, put pen to paper with your ideas, because this commitment will take you to the next level.

Keep going, you got this!

EXERCISE 4:

Create your vision board before moving on – think of the words, images and colours that represent your vision in life.

Some points to think of:

- Do you want to move house?
- Do you want a new job?
- Do you want a new relationship?
- Do you want to buy new clothes?

Have fun making your vision board and get excited about what's to come.

Create a meditation playlist before moving on

Some points to think of:

- What are you trying to work on emotionally?
- Do you prefer meditation music or a person guiding you?

Enjoy your meditation and plan to engage in meditations at the same time each day if you can.

Create a feel-good playlist before moving on

Some points to think of:

- How do you want to feel when listening to your playlist?
- What songs can you pick that reflect this mood?

Listen to your playlist as often as you can.

CHAPTER 5

WAKE UP AND START LIVING

It is time to wake up and start living!

So many people move through each day going over and over the same routine, never really questioning what they do or why they do it. You are reading this book and you are different. You are ready to wake up and really start living! To live life from your purpose is where the magic of life comes in, just like we covered in chapter 1. We all want life to be magical, however a large majority of people are not prepared to do the work that will get them there. It does take work to really live as you will be coming to understand now. You have already started the process of living a magical life as you have taken action by picking up this book. It is important you are aware of this and that you praise yourself for this action as not everyone will do this.

Some of the action steps you have engaged in since starting this book will change how you feel about life and how you interact with others. You have been engaging in some real personal development in Chapters 1 to 4. The content around the magic in life, your wants and desires, healing past pain and building a stronger story is not easy, but here you are continuing to read on so be very proud of yourself. This chapter also has action steps within it, read the whole chapter first and complete exercise 5 at the end of the chapter. Exercise 5 guides you on the action steps and what to do next.

It takes healing past pain, recognising and understanding your intuition, knowing yourself on a deeper level, letting go of the past and building a stronger story to really begin to live our life. This is not to say nothing bad or upsetting will happen to us ever again, but it will mean we will approach it better each time and release it quicker, as opposed to it building up over the years and becoming a huge issue.

When we are working on waking up and starting to really live we are starting to work with our solar plexus, the centre of getting things done. The solar plexus, just to remind you, is the energy centre and is also known as the fire within. When our solar plexus is working well, we are confident, we get things done, we trust in our own transformation. When the solar plexus is not working well, perhaps damaged or underdeveloped, we are like a torch with a low battery, our light has gone out and we show up in life in a dismissive way.

There are some check points to work with to notice if your solar plexus is working well or if it needs work. If you answer no to any of the following, it is an indication that your solar plexus could use an energy boost, and that is what we will work on throughout this chapter.

- I am confident and I show courage in life
- I achieve my goals with limited distractions
- I know my purpose in life and I follow it daily
- I am focused and I am determined

Much of our solar plexus energy centre deals with our sense of identity. Our sense of identity developed within our teen years when we were part of the family unit. In our adult years many of the ways we view ourselves is outdated and it impacts how we live, making it hard for us to truly wake up and live our life.

If you were raised by parents who were focused on perfection, chances are you may struggle to achieve your goals as there is an underlying fear of "what if this doesn't work out", or you may spend more time trying to perfect the smaller details, forgetting the bigger picture.

No matter what you are facing, it is well worth working with the energy of your solar plexus, as this is what builds a good foundation for us to give love and to receive love.

If we want to start living we need to let go of our fear of being seen by others. Many people hide away their talents based on the need for approval from others. This is not us being seen, this is us hiding and crushing our personal power and our joy in life. We want to be confident enough within our own skin to stand up and be seen for who we are. We want to be seen in the world, this being the reason we are on social media, going for promotions in work, reconnecting with old friends, and even reading this book. This is much easier for us to do when we have made peace with the past, because, if we are holding on to past emotional pain, it can infect how we feel about ourselves and cause all sorts of emotional blocks when it comes to being seen.

When our minds are clear we make better decisions around our life direction.

I work with many people who are in the process of wanting to be seen, wanting to let go of the chains that have held them back for so long, and wanting to truly live their purpose. People enter therapy to feel confident about life, and confidence has us showing up in ways that we get things done. We as humans strive for connection with others and, when we are not experiencing true connection, we feel sad and lonely.

One common factor gets in the way – FEAR.

Fear comes in many forms: fear of the unknown, fear of rejection, fear of failure and fear of success. We must get to know our fears and make peace with our fears continuously as we move through the journey of life. When my clients want to be seen and are moving through the journey of being seen, I am constantly helping them to learn to listen to what their fears have to say, to understand what work they have to do. Being seen is being heard in your romantic relationship. Being seen is being valued at work. Being seen is belonging in the family unit.

> Have you learned what you want from life?
> Have you started to make peace with the past?
> Have you started to build a stronger story?

Anything you want in life is at the other side of fear and it is important you push through fear because, if you don't, you will still face fears daily and you won't live the magic of life. We have covered a lot in Chapters 1 to 4, however we are always working with ourselves and tuning into our internal guidance system if we want more from life. The hardest parts are always in the early days of the journey, and it does get easier the further you move along the journey.

> What have you learned about yourself by reading Chapters 1 to 4?

Those who are replaying the same day every day will never slow down enough to truly wake up and start living. They will not know who they are, what makes them happy or what direction they are going in. Those who are ready to be awakened will always be aiming to understand themselves better. Those who are living day to day will face fear, disappointment and upset. You want more from life, shown by you finding the courage to pick up this book! It is so much better to face the fears that will take you in the right direction. This is where your power is.

CASE STUDY 4
CARLA AGED 43

Carla is a single parent to 3 children under the age of 10. Carla has recently split with her husband and finds life extremely difficult. Carla finds it difficult to find a positive balance between working and being a parent. Whilst Carla's ex-husband is very supportive, she finds there is huge pressures on her from her family members. Carla's family relationships have been strained since she was a teenager due to family conflict and many members of her family no longer speak to her. Carla feels isolated and lonely a lot of the time.

Carla feels huge pressure from her parents to do her best at all times and feels they are not supportive of her due to her current life situation. Carla's parents do not help her out with childcare, meaning Carla has to juggle a lot in life.

Carla finds daily life a real struggle and constantly feels exhausted. Carla watches friends manage the balance in their life well, but felt like her mood was very low on a daily basis due to parenting 3 young children and trying to make ends meet with money. Carla decided that therapy was the answer, she craved to feel like herself again prior to the pressures of parenting and marital breakdown.

When Carla entered therapy she shared that she felt under pressure to be "perfect" and to get everything right. When we explored this more we found a lot of the pressure was in and around the way Carla's parents reacted towards her. Carla's mum was a successful businesswoman when Carla was growing up, and the family had a good income based *on this. Despite being comfortable with money, Carla shared that her mum would create a lot of pressure around being the best at everything. Carla, whilst reflecting on childhood, was not able to recall any memories of being praised as a child and could only remember feeling shame that her efforts were never good enough. Carla recalled memories of her mum "forcing" her to stay at home to study for exams, meaning she missed out on a lot of social time with friends. Carla brought forward in a therapy session a time when she had achieved 90% in a test and her mum's reaction towards this was questioning why she didn't achieve 100%. Carla had a story within that she had to be perfect to be lovable.*

We unpacked these memories and emotions during therapy, much of the time Carla cried as we did so. Carla didn't want to be perfect, she wanted to be real. We started keeping track of Carla's achievements week to week, noting down what went well and what this meant for Carla and her children. Carla started to recognise that perfection was impossible and that small steps of progress were much healthier to focus on.

Slowly but surely, Carla started to feel better about herself and her relationship with her parents changed. Carla set healthy personal boundaries and no longer aimed to please her parents as she started to put her own happiness first. The boundaries Carla set had made her parents realise that to be part of her

> life, they had to accept her for the way she was. Carla noticed her parents started to help her out more, meaning she had more time for herself and socialising which, Carla felt, is important for a single parent. Carla was more confident in her abilities to balance work and parenting, and shared that she no longer felt low.

Do you resonate with Carla's story at all? If you feel you do, what parts resonate most?

Our stories we hold about ourselves tell people how we want to be treated. When we know and understand these stories, we can set boundaries with people, telling them how we want to be treated. When we do this, even the most difficult family relationships can turn around for the better. Remember, we want to belong to groups, we want to belong in the family, we want to belong in our relationships and we want to belong in work!

You might be thinking, "How can I start to wake up and start living?"

My simple answer is to follow your purpose. Make a decision to follow your heart and to do what you love despite the obstacles that your ego may be throwing up to you. Think back to your wants from Chapter 2, open your heart to receiving those wants. Remember you are working through your journey by working through this book. You have been getting to know yourself better as you have been reading along. You have already started to tap into the magic of life and you have already started to look at what you want from life. Your story is becoming stronger and stronger and stronger the more you heal, the more you relax, and the more you tap into your heart space. You have started to learn about the mind and how it works, and why it is so important to feed your mind with the ideas of what you want in life.

It is now time to really wake up and to start living.

Despite the fears, you have started to take action. Despite the fears, you have started to create your vision board. Despite the fears, you have spent time in meditation. Despite the fears, keep taking action to show up and move to the next level.

You will not get anywhere without action. The time is now!

So, you are now familiar with what you want to bring into your life, and you have started to build your stronger story by setting the foundations through vision boards, meditation and music. Each chapter is as important as the other because it works on each step along the journey, building and building the foundations for emotional success.

Let's live your purpose starting today.

The first place we want to look at is your morning routines to truly wake up and start living.

- What do you do with your morning?
- Do you bring some of your purpose into your morning?

- Are your habits simply habits that you go through without much thought?

Some people do the same thing every morning and it has no positive impact on their day.

I want you to start thinking of ways you can bring more of your purpose into your morning. Remember in Chapter 4 we spoke about habits and how they are created through consistency, reminders and a vision? It is now time to have a look at your morning routine to determine whether or not you are bringing your vision to life.

Let me share a personal experience with you.

Back when I first really started to 'wake up and start living', I started to listen to motivational material in the morning. I started to have a hunger for feeling good. I started to want to feel better in the mornings. I am a morning person so have always felt good in the mornings, however I wanted to feel even better and I made it my goal to listen to motivational content that would add value to my desire each day.

My desire was to build my own business, this was back when I started to ask questions about me, about my life. This was when I was around 27/28 years old. This is the time I started to sense there was more to life. I was feeling crushed working for others and something was telling me there was more light in another place. I knew I had to start working on me to get ready for the next level.

> I must remind you that this journey is not always easy. It is a journey where you have to be willing to look within yourself, like really look within yourself, to recognise the areas that require your attention.

We have been doing this throughout the book, so know that by still reading this book you are showing courage for the journey! To truly live we need to know who we are on a deeper level. You might think this sounds silly, but so many people hold themselves in tense spaces and in tense positions that prevent the magic flowing into their life, meaning they are not allowing themselves to live a fulfilled life.

Around the time of writing this book I had started to look at increasing my work around my own mind and body connection. This was something I had done for a while, but I felt a deep desire to take this a step further.

I started to attend hot yoga on a regular basis. You might ask what hot yoga is. It is simply yoga in a hot room. I found my mind and body connection start to develop on an even deeper level. I found myself becoming more and more intuitive and my inner knowing was flowing like never before. I only had to think of something and then open social media and right in front of me there was a quote, either answering my thought or encouraging the thought I had. I would be reading something and at the exact same time someone would say the words I was reading on the TV. Yes, it does shock me too! I sometimes stop and laugh and shake my head, thinking "wow", and other times I cry tears of joy thinking this is just magical.

I have been working on developing my intuition over the years as I have always had a great interest in signs, energy and even ghosts when I was younger, as I have mentioned before. I used to speak about wanting to work with ghosts. I believe this was the only way I could describe my desire to work with energy. Healing from your past emotional pain creates great space for your intuition to flow. Many people mix up ego and intuition because it can be easy to believe something to be true to fit your story. Intuition is completely different from ego, as it will always come for your greater good. You will be developing and working with your intuition as you move through this book.

Have you noticed yourself become more aware of yourself and your own ideas since reading this book?

We will talk about intuition again as we move through this book. We have to allow ourselves to be in alignment with our new desires and our new way of living, or else we remain in resistance mode and nothing special really happens for us. This is why it is so important to create the vision before taking action. The vision will drive you in your action steps. When you are feeling fear about taking action, reminding yourself of your vision will help you to take those next steps!

A good example of what can happen when you are not in resistance mode is this.

I am starting each day right now with journaling. I do this as soon as I get up and I make it my goal to call in my angels and guides for support, focusing on something particular each day. I work with my angels and guides every day and feel a huge sense of peace with this. I am a very spiritual person and I like to tap into guidance. If this doesn't feel right for you, you can call it your higher self or your best self and so on. You do not have to use the word angels or guides if it doesn't feel right for you, but, know this, there is a power much greater than you can explain at work in this world and, when we tap into it and trust, we truly wake up and we start living.

Earlier in the week I had completed my journaling and had then spent some time writing about the moon in this book, as it was around the full moon cycle. What happened next was lovely. I arrived at hot yoga and the lady had me confused with another Brooke, and the conversation led to a moon ceremony she had arranged and she had thought I had booked in. I told her I hadn't, but I would be booking in immediately. We laughed and smiled about this as I told her I had been writing about the moon that morning. This is the magic of life and it happens when we least expect it, provided we allow it to happen. If I had been in resistance mode this wouldn't have happened. Resistance mode has us walking with our heads down, seeking protection, it doesn't allow for beautiful conversations to be had. We have a choice to either stay in resistance mode or allow ourselves to open up to the magic of life.

How often are you in resistance mode?

You may be working with the moon cycles now too after completing the full moon exercise in Chapter 3. You may also have started to notice beautiful events happening in your life as a result.

Your vision board, your meditation, your feel-good playlist will all help you to open your heart to allowing the magic to come into your life.

All of these steps are your action steps to bring more magic into your life. Without a vision you wander each day never really knowing where you are going. Your actions say "yes" to everyone and anyone, meaning your energy is depleted, leading to exhaustion. Your vision you worked on in Chapters 2 and 4 will help you to wake up to the magic of life and to live it daily.

Are you ready to live a life of magic and purpose?

By working on the action steps in this book the past pain truly becomes a thing of the past and you start to connect with others in deeper and more meaningful ways. This is when your journey really starts to feel real. When you wake up to the magic of life, you will realise how painful it was to be sleeping all of these years. Divine timing has a lot to answer for because you always wake up to the magic of life exactly when you are supposed to. So much of my life is based on trusting the timing and trusting that everything happens for a reason. I say this even when I speak of my most difficult times because I believe they happened to lead me to where I am now. I can say my most difficult times actually arrived to wake me the hell up, because, if they hadn't come and forced me to face my darkest parts, I would still be sleeping. However, I am awake to the absolute magic in life and it feels amazing!

If you are still not there with this feeling, do not worry as you will get there.

You may be reading this kind of book for the very first time and you may have a lot of emotional baggage to release before you feel the magic in life. Rest if you need to, but do not quit! When you have woken up to the magic in life, you will be seen in this world, your light will shine and others will be drawn to you. A lot of my empath clients actually come to me to protect their light because they often feel, when they have woken up, they shine so bright that they become a target for energy vampires. When you shine, people who are a little darker will be drawn to your light and, if you are not careful, they will feed off your light, leaving you drained.

When you wake up and start living you must protect your energy from those who are stealing it.

It is okay to share your light, this is the whole purpose of waking up, but it becomes an issue when you are drained of your light and have nothing left for you. Your meditation practices and holding your vision will help you to protect your light, because having a purpose keeps you focused and helps you to make good choices. However, this alone will not be enough and you will have to work on protecting your mind as you awaken to the magic in life. You are surrounded every single day by words of others, songs, tv programmes, media and so much more, some of which you are hearing may have you coming off track and losing sight of your vision. It is absolutely essential you develop healthy morning routines, healthy eating routines and healthy bedtime routines to stay on track.

> Going back to your morning routines, it is important that you develop good habits that keep you focused and to start your day from the best place.

What I must say is that you do not need to get up at 5am to live an emotionally successful life. I have never gotten up at 5am to work on my ideas. It is important that you create a good start in the day, i.e. being up around 6/7am to make the most of your day. Emotionally successful people tend to use the hours in their day wisely, but it is important to remember that you can do this sensibly and do not need to burn yourself out to do so.

> Let's look at what you can do in your day to start living!

ACTION STEP 4: MORNING ROUTINE:

Developing a healthy morning routine is the best place to start.

You do not need to fill your morning with lots of tasks, this is where a lot of people go wrong. I have clients who come to me really upset and overwhelmed as they have too many tasks to complete in the morning based on personal development ideas. I want to set you free from the worry by making it simple for you. Do one thing each morning that is in alignment with your wants for life. Here is a list to choose from to make it easier for you:

- Listen to a motivational video
- Read a few pages of a personal development book
- Meditate on your vision
- Breathe deeply and visualise yourself already living in accordance with your wants
- Listen to a feel-good playlist
- Write your desire out with pen and paper as though it has already happened

> *This is just a guide to get started and you will be able to add more to this list.*

Your main aim is to have one thing in your morning routine that raises your energy and has you taking an action step towards your desires. This morning I was listening to motivational content as I got ready, because I am working on really powering up my self-belief to get this book finished. The motivational content lights my fire within in the mornings and sets me up with an attitude of "I can get this done!"

> *You do not need to be following an overwhelming list in the morning.*

You only need to make sure you engage in one task that will have you taking one action step towards your vision that you created in Chapters 2 and 4. When you start your morning well you set yourself up for a good day, and one good day leads to another, and another, and another. Remember, habits are created when we do something over and over. You will want to start creating good morning habits now.

ACTION STEP 5: EVENING ROUTINE:

The next part of your day you want to master is your evening routine.

The way we close off the day has a huge impact on how we live our life. Our emotional state going to bed has an impact on how we sleep, which has an impact on how we wake the next day. It is important you develop a bedtime routine that incorporates gratitude and thanks for the day that has gone by. This will help you to enter a sleep state with a positive mindset, which will allow you to rest easily and set yourself up in the best possible way for a good day upon awakening. Just like the morning routine, your bedtime routine doesn't have to be filled with overwhelming tasks, it simply has to have a little bit of time set aside to develop and practice an attitude of gratitude.

Here is a list of some ideas you can bring into your bedtime routine:

- Meditation
- Affirmations for a good night's sleep
- Write down 3 parts of your day that went well and why, bringing in some positive emotions

- Listen to relaxing music
- Switch off all electronics 30 minutes before sleep to allow your mind and body to wind down

These are just some suggestions to try, you can add your own to this list too. The most important part of this is that you start to engage in good habits in the morning and in the evening *today*, to start and end your day in a magical way. You will be noticing again that living your life in the best possible way takes a little effort on your part, but, when you develop the habits, they will start to feel really natural to you and you will find they become habits you cannot live without.

Waking up to life is about engaging with your heart space and your life desires.

When you wake up you become conscious of the habits you engage in. Ensure your habits serve your life purpose because, otherwise, you will live your life in exhaustion and despair and panic and fear, day in and day out. To truly live your purpose is to become mindful of how you show up daily, and to really understand yourself on a deeper level. I live my life on my purpose daily and, although this does not mean that fear does not creep in sometimes, I can deal with it better as I have my morning routines, my bedtime routines, my meditation, my vision board and so on. All of these routines and visions protect us in some way and help us to make good choices that are in alignment with our life path.

When we wake up and start living, our relationships feel better, our career feels better, we laugh more, we feel more connected to others, we enjoy our free time, we work well under pressure, we feel real, and we rest well. You may already be starting to notice such changes in your life by starting to follow the action steps in this book. Remember it is a working progress, so be patient with yourself and revisit certain parts of this book as and when needed. You can jump back to certain chapters if you feel you need to hear the messages again, in particular the parts of the book that you felt spoke to you. Whilst it is good to reflect, it's not good to get stuck there, so keep moving forward alongside reflecting. Also try to avoid skipping parts of the book as this will not work in your favour. Just like a house is built from strong foundations, you must also build this life journey with strong foundations. So, move through this book bit by bit, following the exercises as you go and revisiting chapters or exercises if you need to.

EXERCISE 5:

- Create a morning and evening routine – write out each routine and place it next to your bed to ensure you will see it often.

- Take some time out to think of what you have learned about yourself so far. What improvements have you made? What is still getting in your way of emotional success?

CHAPTER 6

WHEN IT ALL FEELS STUCK AGAIN

Life can easily become stuck again, no matter how much work you have put in to get things going in the right direction.

You may have followed all the action steps in this book, from creating a vision board to making a playlist to meditating, yet something is still missing. Know and trust that this is okay. It is okay for us to feel stuck again.

If you are feeling stuck, stop for a moment, breathe deep and place one hand on your heart centre and the other on your tummy. Ask yourself the question, "What do I need to let go of to feel good?" Be patient and sit for a few moments to see what comes up for you. You can do this any time you are stuck, and you can sit for as long as you feel you need to.

Life is life and we become stuck from time to time; however, by reading this book, it will mean you will not come off track for long.

The longer you are off track with your life's intentions, the more emotional discomfort builds up. The breathing action above will help you to realign when you feel stuck. You will also be able to get back on track soon by reading this chapter and tapping into your internal resources. Try when life hits hard to keep on track as much as you can with your intentions and life purpose. The good thing is, if you are living your purpose, it will pull you in the right direction as opposed to you having to push it.

One of the greatest gifts of life is that we are often both our problem and our solution.

We are the ones who actually hold ourselves back in life a lot by resisting the good, and we do a lot of this by not speaking our truth. I have had many clients over the years come to me for help in speaking their truth. It's not an easy thing to do, especially in today's world where the fear of hurting others is very strong. We can learn to speak our truth in kindness to avoid becoming stuck over and over again.

Often people who are not speaking their truth will suffer from sore throats, sore ears, sore shoulders and sore necks, this is as a result of tensions building around the throat area. Also, sore ears are a sign of not speaking the truth or an unwillingness to hear the truth. If you really tune in with your body, you will get to know your own body and the signs it is sending to you. Many of our physical tensions, aches and pains are a manifestation of mental challenges or unhealed traumas. We work a lot with this in therapy sessions.

What truths in your life are you ignoring or refusing to hear?

I often experience blocked ears. When this happens, my hearing becomes muffled and I can hear quieter noises much louder. It was very strange at first, but I came to realise, after it happening several times over the years, that this happens to me when I am ready to move up to the next level with my goals and intentions. It's almost like my hearing shuts down to clear old energy to get ready for the new. I once saw a DR about it in the early stages and she called me a "medical mystery". This was at the time I was unsure what was happening and initially I thought I had a medical issue. Anyway, after 3 visits and nothing to find I told the DR what I was starting to sense and her response was, "Brooke there is a lot of things that happen in life that the medical profession cannot explain". This was the last time I saw a DR for this as I started to trust something was happening and I would soon know the answers. Now, I know when it happens and what comes next.

Have you ever experienced anything similar to this?

It can be easy to become stuck again when we are on our personal development journey, and it can be even easier to become even more stuck when we get stuck with being stuck. Often, when we become stuck, we start to resist the feelings of being stuck, which means we start to go head-to-head with the feelings of being stuck, creating conflict within. Remember, this is a journey and it will have it ups and downs. It is important that you embrace those ups and downs and become the student when it feels like you are in a downward spiral.

Our down times and our struggles have come to teach us.

Our tough times come to teach us about the parts of ourselves that require our attention. When writing this chapter, for the last few days I have felt a little struggle and tension arise as a result of something in my personal life I have been working on. I have learned over the years that sometimes when this comes up it is good to have an early night and just go to bed rather than fighting against the struggle. The past 2 nights I have gone to bed early to ensure I am getting enough rest to be able to learn through this struggle. I have been journaling every morning for the past 6 weeks which has helped massively as, even in this struggle, I am still feeling a calmness. Before, I would have felt heightened anxiety during times of struggle and I would have been searching and searching for the answers immediately.

Patience has been something I have been practicing for the past few years and I feel I have almost mastered this.

I have been checking in with myself and really asking *why* I am feeling such a calmness in the face of struggle. The answer that keeps coming back to me is that the journaling, tapping into my emotional state regularly, is keeping me in touch with my higher self, which is creating a trust in the belief that all will be okay. I am really feeling these words as I type them and really feeling engaged with my heart chakra energy. I am in no way saying this is simple and easy, but, if you follow the steps in this book, you can achieve this sense of calm in your struggles too.

You may be thinking, "why do we struggle" and "why does it come back up when we have made peace with the past and when we know what we want?"

Reading this book will not prevent future struggles in life or challenging situations. However, it will provide you with the tools to manage and navigate through these tough times. We wouldn't want to stop the struggle appearing because the struggle teaches us what we need to know, to learn about ourselves and to live an emotionally successful life.

Let me explain this more.

Struggle, in fact let's call it different ways of looking at life, are a part of life itself. When we are in struggle, we are often looking at something in a way that holds us in the struggle. We are often looking at our stickiness as opposed to solutions. Being in the stickiness can have many benefits so long as we don't stay there too long. Being in the stuck zone highlights to us that something has arisen that we need to make a choice on or that we need to heal. When we understand this, we are better equipped to make a good choice that allows us to progress forward. Sitting with our struggle or different viewpoints and examining them with a curiosity helps us to learn about ourselves. We can always refer back to the breathing technique at the start of this chapter when we feel stuck for insight and guidance.

Curiosity when facing struggle helps us to open up to new ways of looking at our situation.

Curiosity helps us to be creative and may actually help us to move forward quicker than we have before. Getting curious and being open minded to different solutions can help a situation to move forward faster. A lot of people can become extremely stubborn in times of struggle and can keep themselves there for long periods of time. When I am working with my clients, often they share with me how much they value their sessions in times of struggle, because their times of struggle are a lot shorter when we're working together as opposed to before when we weren't. In sessions where a client is facing a challenge after moving forward, we approach it with curiosity to understand what is best to do to get the situation moving again. This can be far more freeing than you may believe right now.

The last thing you want to do when you face challenges is to get creative, but that is what will get you out of the challenge and on your way to living your best life again.

I have been having conversations recently with many people who are very unclear about what they want in life. I am very clear on what I want and was starting to find struggle within me as to why these conversations keep appearing. I was starting to question what is going on within me that I am attracting such conversations. I have been sitting with this for days and I have been trusting that, when the time is right, I will hear the answer. This morning this happened for me, the answer arrived. I was listening to a personal development clip this morning as I do every morning and the person spoke about when we recognise a difference between us and others, we know that we have changed.

This was a penny dropping moment for me and the dark clouds of struggle parted as I heard these words.

I stopped what I was doing so I could feel the words too. I dropped into my feeling zone to really understand what these words had meant to me. I understood that I was recognising this because I had become super clear on what I wanted, and I realised that actually these conversations were dropping away fast. I was using my intuition as I just knew I was supposed to hear these words on this day.

Do you ever have penny dropping moments like this?

These conversations had appeared to help me realise that I had changed. I was no longer trying to change the vibe of others by helping them to see what they wanted. I had become the observer and had recognised these people were in a learning zone themselves and they did not need my input, their journey is their own. My job was to recognise that I was no longer trying to hold on to that which did not serve me, and I was simply observing and letting it flow. Previously, I would have allowed my energy to become wrapped up in the confusion, not allowing myself to see clearly, but I had realised, in these words I heard this morning, that I had moved on and these conversations had appeared to show me I had broken an unhealthy pattern. I felt instantly proud of my efforts and the struggle was no more. The calmness totally took over.

What actions have you taken since reading this book that leaves you feeling proud of yourself?

For me this could have been a different outcome had I not allowed myself to be open to the answers coming. It could have been a different outcome had I not allowed myself the rest to be open to the answers. Do you see how our morning and bedtime routines impact our ability to learn our life lessons? Even when you are facing challenges, I urge you to stick with your new habits, and to stick to them even more, and they will help you so much. Some people think that our habits are only required when we are struggling, but we want to commit to them daily, even on the good days, to ensure positive momentum is maintained and your life keeps moving forward to the magic of life.

It could have been a different outcome had I become stuck with feeling, stuck creating more and more resistance. There are times other people's actions are showing us areas of ourselves that need our attention, and there are times other people's actions appear to show us how far we have come. When we understand our own story, we have the knowledge to know what the situation is trying to tell us. It has taken me some time to trust my inner knowing and to work with my 3rd eye energy (intuition) to fully know the ins and outs of the situation, but to get to this stage is simply beautiful. When we work with our intuition we start to see things in life clearly.

> You are taking steps towards this too
> by reading this book.

As I write this part of the book regarding my recent struggle and lesson, we are in the midst of the Leo full moon, which is a time of big lessons and connection with our emotional state. The full moon can throw up all sorts of emotions for us, and over the past few years I have been consciously working with the cycles and getting in tune with the energy. I trust that working with the moon cycles has had a significant impact on my healing journey, and that the moon's energy helped me in this situation that I was stuck in. You may be finding already that the full moon exercise from Chapter 3 has helped you to start working with the moons energy and your own emotional guidance system.

We as humans work in cycles and it is important that we understand this to allow ourselves the gift of working with and through the cycles, always learning more and more about ourselves. Many people reach out to me around the time of the full moon due to the heightened emotions they are feeling and the fear of them. Of course, it is going to be scary when your emotions are rising and you do not know what to do with them, or when life feels stuck again. It can be scary and very frustrating. This is why it is super important to make peace with your past, to be able to remove the emotional intensity from past memories to ensure you are able to move forward with a sense of calm and a sense of curiosity. When pain resurfaces, it is important to repeat the healing cycle again to clear out any emotions, memories or negative thoughts you may have missed.

Hitting a brick wall again in your journey is natural as it is a journey with twists and turns, but it is always providing opportunities to learn more and more about yourself. Work with the challenges, let go of the resistance and flow with the lessons, allowing yourself to reach new levels of life. Be okay with where you are at even when times are tough, but make a commitment to yourself to keep working with your emotions and to keep understanding yourself.

You may want to revisit your list of wants from life to gain a deeper understanding of what may have gone wrong. Revisiting your wants may remind you of what you have been doing to take you off track. Revisiting your wants and desires in life is a continual process. The list you made in Chapter 2 will be a list you will revisit over and over again, it will be your go to list when times are good to remind yourself of how far you have come, and it will be your go to list when times are tough to remind yourself of ways to get yourself back on track.

Are you still in alignment with the wants you committed to earlier in the book?

Remember, it is very easy to come off track as we live in a fast-paced world with so many people looking for and needing our attention. It may be that you have let your morning routine slip, or it may be you have not been meditating as much as you had been when everything was going well. Sitting with your challenges with an open mind, and reminding yourself of what you are working towards, will help you to become stronger and wiser.

> You will find yourself keen to get back on track because you will have developed a better relationship with yourself from working through this book.

One day not so long ago you may have fallen into a habit of putting yourself last. However, now you may be noticing that you are putting yourself first more and more. You will no longer stand for unhappiness or failure, you will see the opportunities in front of you and you will work with them in a way that helps you to feel super about yourself.

> The way we treat ourselves becomes the way others treat us.

> How are others treating you? Are there changes you need to make to your personal boundaries?

If we are putting ourselves last all the time, chances are others will put us last too. It is time to put yourself first again when you hit those challenging times. It is time to revisit the vision board when you hit those challenging times. It is time to turn the playlist up when you hit those challenging times. It is time to meditate more when you hit those challenging times, because this is what will get you through it.

Sometimes when clients finish their therapy journey they return again soon after, because they realise there was a challenge they did not go deep enough with and they feel that they need to revisit it. It may be good for you to return to this chapter when you feel challenges arising again. This will encourage further healing to take place and will add even more value to your self-development journey. I spoke about curiosity before, re-reading this chapter feeds your curious mind and each time you will take something more from this, like my clients do when they return to therapy. Also, re-reading will help you to understand on an even deeper level the steps you have taken for yourself and your life since reading this book. You can never read self-development material enough. Each time you refer back to the material any resistance you may be holding on to will dissolve even more.

Remember, divine timing plays a role in this journey, and trust that if something resurfaces it was supposed to resurface for further healing.

EXERCISE 6

- Revisit your *why* when you feel stuck, remind yourself of *why* you started this book and what you hoped to achieve – go back to your list from Chapter 2, are you completely in alignment with your wants and desires or do you need to make slight changes?

- Take a look at your vision board, do you need to add or remove something from the board to make it feel better?

- Revisit your meditation playlists, are they working, do they need a change? Do you need to meditate more?
- Is your music causing more sadness than happiness?
- Is your morning routine working? If not, make some changes.
- Is your bedtime routine working? If not, make some changes.

Work with this list and spend time thinking about your wants, your action and the challenges you still face. We will continue to work on this as we move through the rest of the book. This chapter has created space to really review what you have been working on, to fine tune the parts of your exercises that need to be altered, and has been a guide to help you get the most out of the action steps in Chapter 4 and Chapter 5.

You are well along your way to experiencing the magic of life – keep going!

CHAPTER 7

TRUST IN THE JOURNEY OF LIFE

Well done for arriving at Chapter 7, you have been challenging yourself throughout this book and you have made a commitment to yourself, despite it being difficult to keep going.

> You are truly starting to tap into
> your inner warrior!

Throughout this book we have been looking at ways to make life more magical by knowing exactly what we want from life and our desires. By now you will be more aware that to fully live your life you must process and heal emotional hurts. By doing this we can then take action to build our stronger story and to live life from this new, empowered place. In the chapters that came before, you challenged yourself to get to know yourself on a deeper level, understanding your desires in life but also understanding and encouraging the healing that needs to take place before achieving these desires. The action steps have been helping you to really power up the magic in your life, to bring to you the experiences in life you truly deserve.

In this chapter we will focus on what it means to trust the journey of life as we make our way along our personal development journey.

The most important thing we can do is trust in the journey of life, even when times are tough. I know only too well how hard it can be to trust in the journey of life when life is tough. It can be very difficult to follow the action steps in Chapter 4 and 5 when it seems like the world is out to get you and when emotions are running high. There are occasions where we need to take the leap of faith and trust that everything will work out. We must keep following the action steps in order to push through the emotional times to create more and more trust in our lives.

Many of the clients who come to me are desperate to build trust for their life and to believe deeply that it will all work out, no matter how hard it is. When entering a therapy journey, the first step is encouraging the individual to develop a sense of trust in themselves and in the process of life. The case study below will provide an example of this.

CASE STUDY 5
ALANA AGED 48

Alana is a successful career woman in finance, managing a team of 5 people. Alana loved her job but felt something was missing. Alana's manager would ask her to do more and more at work and Alana, despite feeling successful and enjoying her job, started to notice the pressure was getting to her. Alana missed social events due to taking her workload home. Alana's line manager never thanked her for the work she put in and, after spending a lot of weekends working in her own time, Alana felt something had to change.

Alana engaged in an intense therapy programme as she felt she had to explore her work life balance and the pressure she was under at work. Alana explained she was here seeking a deep sense of trust in herself, to develop a self-belief and self-love to combat the pressures and negative words from her boss. Whilst discussing Alana's challenges, we noticed that Alana's work environment was very toxic and Alana often spent a great deal of time listening to other people's problems. Alana recognised, whilst exploring this in a therapy session, that no one appreciated the time and effort she put into her work, both personally and professionally.

Looking back to what life was like as a child, Alana explored the fact that her mum raised her and her 3 siblings on her own, often working long hours to make ends meet. Alana remembered her mum speaking about there not being enough hours in the day to work and struggling to make ends meet. Alana remembered her mum being a very hard worker, but often speaking about no one appreciating her. The realisation that Alana was living her mum's life over again hit Alana hard. Alana shared that she had to face some real hard truths in therapy, as she hadn't realised just how much her line manager was taking advantage of her kindness, as she named it.

Alana explored what it means now to have a work life balance and to be appreciated. We looked at areas of Alana's life where she was appreciated and a lot of that was at home by her partner. We focused a lot about what it meant to be appreciated and how it felt. This was a way of helping Alana recognise that appreciation in the workplace was just as important.

Alana decided during our time together that a move to a new workplace was vital. Alana had developed a huge sense of trust in herself to take action to improve her life, despite what others thought of her. Alana started to look for workplaces that value an employee's time and effort, and a flexible working pattern was important for Alana. Due to Alana's sheer determination and the work we did around appreciation, Alana found herself a new job with better terms and recognised quickly her new workplace was like a home from home. Alana felt more relaxed, more appreciated and a lot better about life in general.

We are not always aware when we have picked up the habits of the adults we were brought up with, especially when the patterns are destructive. Alana was not aware when she came to therapy that she had picked up negative habits from her mum and was replaying her mum's life. Alana had to begin to trust herself as a mature adult to make the necessary changes in her life that would lead to improvements. The adults in our life mean well, just like Alana's mum had, and do the best they can with what they have, but, without realising it as children, we pick up on their bad habits at times and play this out in our own adult years. When we spend time exploring our story, we can recognise bad habits to change our story to one of emotional success and inner peace.

Can you resonate with Alana's story at all? Are there bad habits you have picked up from the adults you grew up around?

When I think back to the tough times I have had in life, such as my divorce, awful relationship breakdowns, having to start all over again several times, I remember always having a sense of hope and trust, even when my heart was aching. I have had several tough times in my adult years, after many of which it would have been so easy for me to lose all trust in life. But I kept going and I held my vision and for that reason I am able to write this book.

We all have a vision tucked away inside us and you have started to take those initial steps by reading this book.

It won't always be easy and, as you move along this journey, you will have to remind yourself of the magic in life. You will have to release hurt again, because we live in a world where we can be hurt again, and you will have to make a conscious effort to wake up and live every day. Following the action steps in this book will help you to continue to build upon your trust in yourself, and will help you to live an emotionally successful life.

To fully trust in the process of life we have to connect with our mind and body on a regular basis.

Over the past few months, at the time of writing this book, I have started to look after myself more. I felt the urge to increase my mind and body connection and, let me tell you, it has paid off. Our tummy area is like our second brain and will guide us, telling us if something feels right and if it doesn't feel right. This is our area where we start to develop trust with ourselves. We have to work with our emotions regularly to develop that sense of trust. Our emotions sit within our tummy and our emotions are always guiding us to what needs to be worked on within us.

Do you listen to what your emotions are telling you?

A lot of the time people cannot interact with this as they are filled with self-punishment, which leads to guilt and we, as humans, hold on to guilt. It is so painful that we project it out onto others. Instead of recognising what needs to be changed in our life, we see what needs to be changed in others. Guilt is very painful for us to hold on to, and this challenge will leak out into our personal relationships, this being the reason it is so important to work with and heal guilt.

The world will show you in others what needs to be healed in yourself.

The world acts as a large mirror, but often we deny this until it becomes far too painful and we need to do something about it. I would urge you to revisit and re-read this book over and over and follow the steps over and over. I have a few personal development books that I really enjoy and I re-read them, each time taking away something new. I have written this book in a step-by-step way to help you understand your own story. It is not written as a one-off read, it has been written to be read again and again, helping you to become more patient with yourself along the journey.

Patience is a big part of my practice right now, will you allow it to be a big part of yours?

We live in a world where everything goes so fast. We send a text and can see if it has been delivered and read. We send an email and can have a quick response. We have same day delivery on items online. No wonder we find it hard to develop patience. But, as they say, good things come to those who wait. By following the action steps in this book, you will start to practice patience and will become more aware of when you are being impatient or falling into resistance mode. When you notice these negative emotions and feelings coming up, you will be able to move beyond them much quicker.

We are here on a life path that is completely individual to us.

Our own life is working out for us exactly how it is meant to, even more so when we are in a place of trust. When we push the journey of life, we can make mistakes and go down the wrong path, which can add huge amounts of time on to our desired outcomes. When we have started on our journey of knowing what we want, removing the blocks and living a better life, it is essential we develop patience and trust.

> Patience and trust is what allows our journey to unfold.

EXERCISE 7:

- Where do you need to trust more in your life?
- Who do you need to trust more in life?
- What do you do to build your trust?

Make some notes in your journal on these questions to deepen your relationship with trust and faith. In this chapter I have spoken a lot about trusting the journey and by focusing on this it will help you to develop your trust even further. We can always have a little more trust in our journey through life.

CHAPTER 8

WHAT COMES NEXT?

You have taken an extraordinary journey of personal development as you have moved through this book and you owe yourself a massive congratulations. Throughout this book, you will have learned so much about your wants from life, areas of your life that requires healing and how you can take those next steps to living a fulfilled life.

You now have tools to work with to make your life magical, such as your vision board, your meditation and your choice of words. In this chapter you will start to look at what comes next after this book. It is really important when you are on a journey of self-development that you think ahead. Whilst it is good to be mindful, it is also good to be aware of the bigger picture as part of your focus.

I was working with a client this week who has begun to start thinking ahead. We spoke about this in our session as this was not something the client had always done, but, through developing a deeper understanding of themselves, they have been able to know what they need and can now plan ahead to reduce challenges. The trick is to not think too far ahead as this can cause stress or upset. Mindful future planning is key.

What have you learned about yourself by reading this book?

Have you learned anything about yourself that has surprised you?

Has anything you have learned left you feeling excited?

Has anything you have learned left you feel scared?

You will have a bit of everything going on and that is okay. It is important that you remember to make peace with your pain to ensure it does not take over and start to control you. The journey of getting to know yourself will continue now as you will have a keen thirst for it.

By reading this book you have proven you are serious about you.

How we treat ourselves sets the bar for how others treat us. If we are always running late, feeding ourselves last, putting off our own personal development and so on, others will treat us in a way that mirrors this. You will find that others will start to take you more serious now because you will have started to create boundaries, sending a message to them of how you want to be treated. When we start to make ourselves a priority and when we start to truly look after ourselves, others start to have a positive level of respect for us.

> Remember the world acts as a mirror and the energy we put out there comes back to us multiplied.

I have seen clients change the way they carry themselves at the end of their personal development journey. They start to have a positive presence and their body language displays this. Do not mistake this with ego and engaging in actions that will walk over others to get things done, as this is not what I am referring to. Those who have engaged in personal development for the right reasons move on to be positive role models, positive parents, positive partners, positive leaders and so on. The presence is about getting things done in a loving way that benefits all involved.

You may be feeling your whole body and mind has changed since reading this book and, if you haven't yet, stop for a moment and have a think about where you were at when you first started reading this book. Think of all the things that have changed since reading this book. Think about your new habits, your new love for yourself and your new found freedom from emotional pain. Notice the way your personal and professional relationships have changed since reading this book.

> You are well on your way to a wonderful life.

There may also be a sadness rising within you as you draw to the end of this book, this is completely natural. A lot of clients experience the same sadness when they come to the end of therapy. This may happen despite how successful your journey has been. You may have made so much progress, yet still experience this sadness. I want you to know this is okay. You will have been understanding throughout this book that what you feel is what you feel, so it is important to understand your feelings and to hear them with compassion.

The way I work with this at the end of a therapy journey is we stagger the ending. For example, if a client has signed up for 6 weeks and we come to week 5, we may agree to book week 6 in for a few weeks' time, to ensure the ending does not come as a shock and the client feels emotionally prepared. For you as the reader of this book, an important point to remember is that you can read this book as many times as you wish, coming to the end of the book doesn't have to mean it's the end. I revisit the same personal development books over and over. This is far more important than reading for the sake of reading.

You have started to really understand your mind, body and soul through this book. You have started to understand your energy and how your mind and body works with your energy systems. This will really help you in life and will help you to continue to grow and develop as you go.

Keep working with your wants, your desires, your vision and your mind reprogramming exercises. If you give up, you will end up back where you started. The new habits you have started to create will continue to help you, so long as you continue to follow them.

It might be now that you have a keen desire to look at your next steps in life.

You may want to make a new vision board depending on the time that has passed since you worked on your first vision board. No matter how long it has taken you to read this book, know and trust that you have completed this in the time it was supposed to take you and that your actions have been divinely guided.

You are far stronger than you think and you are far more courageous than you often believe!

I could not have wrote this book if it was not for my own desire for more and for the people I have around me that support me and encourage me. This book has been written at the perfect time and I am eternally grateful that you have taken the time to read it.

ABOUT THE AUTHOR

The Empathic Psychologist, Brooke Longmore, is a Mindset and Mental Health Specialist. She has 17 years of experience helping adults, teenagers, children, those in the education system and employed in businesses overcome the obstacles in their lives to live an emotionally successful life. Brooke is due to start an MSc in Forensic Psychological Studies in October 2022, adding to her list of countless qualifications and training courses which cover a wide range of therapies, counselling and spiritual healing.

Understanding Your Own Story is Brooke's first personal development book, which helps adult women overcome the past events and habits that prevents them from having emotionally successful relationships with love, family and work. She has already started planning her second book, Understanding Your Own

Life Journey, which will focus on helping teenagers develop confidence.

Brooke would like to thank you from the bottom of her heart for taking the time to read her first book. She invites you to follow her on social media. You can find Brooke on Facebook, LinkedIn, Twitter, Instagram and TikTok. If you would like to chat with Brooke directly, please contact her by email at:

brooke@brookelongmore.co.uk.

www.ingramcontent.com/pod-product-compliance
Lightning Source LLC
Chambersburg PA
CBHW030303100526
44590CB00012B/500